WAKE UP TOMORROW

A Journey From Darkness To Light

VENUS CHANDLER

©Copyright 2026

IBG Publications, Inc.

Published by I.B.G. Publications, Inc., a Power to Wealth Company

Web address: www.ibgpublications.com

admin@ibgpublications.com / 904-419-9810

Copyright, 2026 by Venus Chandler

IBG Publications, Inc., Jacksonville, FL

ISBN: 978-1-971850-16-0

Chandler, Venus
Wake Up Tomorrow: A Journey From Darkness To Light.

Printed in the United States of America.

DEDICATION

To God: for holding me when I could not hold myself. For breathing life into me when I wanted to stop breathing, and for carrying me through the darkness I thought would end me.

To the girl I once was: who felt invisible, unwanted, hurting, and alone. Thank you for surviving nights that tried to silence you. We made it. This is your victory, your voice, your healing.

To every survivor who cried quietly, who smiled to hide the pain, who pretended to be strong while breaking inside; this book is your hand to hold in the dark.

To anyone reading this who has ever whispered, "I don't want to wake up tomorrow," I pray these pages remind you that you matter, you are needed, you are loved, and you are worthy of staying.

This book was written for the ones still fighting, for the broken hearted and the brave, for those who almost gave up, but chose to breathe one more day.

May these words meet you in your midnight and help you live to see your sunrise.

VENUS CHANDLER

TABLE OF CONTENTS

ACKNOWLEDGMENTS

This book was not written alone. It was carried by grace, held by faith, and born from survival.

First, I give glory to God. For every breath on nights I didn't want to breathe. For every sunrise after the storm. For the strength to wake up tomorrow, again and again. Thank You for never letting go of me, even when I let go of myself.

To my younger self...
Thank you for surviving.
Thank you for staying when you believed you couldn't.
Thank you for holding on long enough to see the woman you would become.

To my family, my children, my husband, and everyone who believed in me, even when I struggled to believe in myself, your love planted seeds that became chapters. Thank you for patience through my silence, grace during my breaking process, and support during my rise.

To the women who have walked this journey with me: sisters in strength, shoulders in seasons of weariness, I honor your courage and your truth. Thank you for reminding me that healing is not meant to be done alone.

To the survivors who held onto breath just one more night, to the readers who come to these pages with trembling hands, to the ones who feel unseen, unheard, or unworthy, this book exists because you exist. Because you deserve to stay, and you deserve tomorrow.

To every friend, mentor, therapist, faith leader, and soul who poured into me at any stage of my healing, your voice echoed when mine trembled.

To anyone who has ever donated, listened, prayed, shared, supported, or believed in this mission, you are part of this story. Your fingerprints are on every page.

And lastly, to the angels we lost too soon. This book is for you too. May our words save the lives you deserved to keep.

Thank you to each heart, seen or unseen, that made this book possible.

A FINAL NOTE FROM THE AUTHOR

If no one told you today, I am honored that you made it this far.

Thank you for trusting these pages with your pain.
Thank you for staying through the memories that burned.
Thank you for choosing breath when silence felt easier.

I wrote this book because I needed it once.
I wrote it for the girl I used to be and for the one reading this now.

You are not alone.
You are not forgotten.
You are not beyond repair.

Healing is not loud, it is consistent.
Gentle.
Patient.
Yours.

I pray you learn to love yourself fully.
I pray joy returns like sunrise, slowly, but surely.
I pray tomorrow feels possible.
And I pray you stay long enough to see the beauty coming for you.

With all my heart,
Thank you for staying.

Coach Venus Chandler

VENUS CHANDLER

Venus Chandler is a survivor, speaker, life coach, and advocates for trauma healing and suicide awareness. After enduring childhood abuse, a suicide attempt at thirteen, and years of silent suffering, she found her voice and purpose through faith, healing, and restoration.

Venus now uses her story to guide women through breakthroughs, boundary-setting, emotional recovery, and rediscovery of self-worth. She founded **Kintsugi Transformations Enterprise**, a healing-centered nonprofit dedicated to empowering women and youth to rebuild their lives with gold in the cracks.

She lives her life as a testament that tomorrow is worth staying for.

There was one night I will never forget. That night, I truly believed the world would be better without me. A night when breathing felt heavy, hope felt far away, and every reason to live was drowned out by the pain inside my chest. I did not want to die; I just wanted the hurt to stop. I wanted silence. I wanted peace. I wanted to escape. And in that moment, suicide whispered to me like a solution.

People think suicide is loud, dramatic, obvious, visible. But mine was quiet. Silent like a tear that never leaves the eye. It was the kind of pain you carry behind a smile, behind responsibilities, or behind "I'm okay." I was functioning. I was showing up. I was surviving. But inside, I was sinking.

I struggled with suicidal thoughts for years. Days when getting out of bed felt like lifting a mountain. Nights when sleep was my only relief.

Times when I questioned my purpose, my worth, and my existence. When darkness feels familiar long enough, it starts to feel like home. And that is a frightening place to be living, but not alive.

My attempt was not dramatic. There were no goodbyes, no letters, no warnings. Just a moment when the weight became too heavy to hold alone. But God had other plans. Something interrupted me, a sound, a thought, a memory, a voice that said, "Not like this." A whisper that reminded me that tomorrow could still look different. I didn't know how to believe that yet, but something inside me held on just long enough.

***

I was thirteen years old, a child by age, but life had forced me into an emotional adulthood far too soon.

We lived in the projects then. The kind of place where walls were thin, secrets were thick, and pain had a way of settling into the cracks of everyday life. I remember the bathroom that night, small, dim, cold tile under my feet.

The mirror staring back at me like it knew my pain but couldn't speak it. I saw a girl I barely recognized. A girl who felt unloved. Unwanted. Invisible. A girl who convinced herself she was ugly, broken, fat and never enough.

I had been abused, physically, mentally, emotionally, and sexually. Trauma was my shadow. Silence was my language. Every day I carried wounds that no one bandaged, questions no one answered, and tears no one noticed. I felt like I was living in a world where love passed me by and left me standing alone. At thirteen, I was already tired. Not teenage-angry tired. Soul tired. Life tired.

One night, overwhelmed and numb, I reached for a bottle of pills. My hands didn't shake. I wasn't crying. I wasn't dramatic. I was empty, and emptiness could feel like calm right before the storm. I took pill after pill quietly, almost mechanically, like I had already disappeared inside myself. I walked to my bedroom afterward and laid down, hoping the pain would leave with my last breath.

My thoughts whispered like poison:
"Nobody loves me."
"I don't belong here."
"Maybe they'll be happier without me."
"I just want peace."
"I can't take anymore."
"I hope I don't wake up tomorrow."

I didn't want to die, I wanted relief. I wanted silence. I wanted to stop hurting. I wanted someone to notice I was drowning without having to scream for help. Sleep felt like the escape I was searching for.

But the next morning... I opened my eyes.

My stomach twisted with sickness, my head heavy, my heart heavier. Instead of relief, I felt disappointed. Anger, even. I was still here. Still hurting. Still invisible. I kept that night to myself like a shameful secret tucked deep in my chest. No one knew. No one asked, so I continued life as if I hadn't just tried to erase myself. I didn't know then that waking up, even angry, even sick, even disappointed, was the first miracle of my story.

I couldn't imagine that the same broken girl who wanted the pain to end would one day write a book to help others hold on. That she would learn to heal, to love herself, to stand tall in her truth. That she would find purpose in the very pain that once convinced her she didn't deserve to live.

This book is not written from a place of perfection or from someone who has everything figured out. It is written from a place of survival. From someone who has been to the edge, looked over, and somehow found her way back. I write this for the version of me who needed someone to say the words I never heard, *"You are not alone". "You are not weak". "You are not hopeless". "And you are needed here."*

I am writing this for anyone who is fighting a battle no one knows about. For the person who is showing up for work, for family, for church, for life, while silently crumbling on the inside. For the one who is smiling in pictures but screaming in the dark. For the one who feels invisible, exhausted, forgotten, or unworthy of love. For the one planning to give up, even while no one suspects a thing.

Suicide is unpredictable. It does not look the same on everyone. It does not discriminate. It arrives through heartbreak, trauma, silence, shame, exhaustion, depression, grief, pressure, rejection, and even loneliness. It wears many masks, and some of the strongest people you know are fighting battles you could never imagine.

If you are reading this and you feel like you are at the end of yourself, I want to say something to you gently but urgently:

Please wake up tomorrow.
Because there is more to your story.
Because tomorrow holds what today cannot see.

Because pain is real, but so is healing.
Because your life still has chapters left to be written.

This book will not tell you to just "be strong" or "think positive." It will sit with you in the dark and remind you that light is still possible. It will walk through the truth of suicide, not with judgment, but with honesty and compassion. It will explore the thoughts we don't say out loud, the warning signs we miss, and the hope that can pull us through another sunrise.

I survived, and I stayed. And if my story can help even one person hold on a little longer, then every tear, every night I wanted to give up, every moment I questioned my existence, becomes part of a purpose bigger than the pain.

So let us begin this journey together, carefully, gently, yet courageously.

Turn the page.
Take a breath.
You are still here.
And the world is better because of it.

"Even the darkest night will end and the sun will rise."

− Victor Hugo

Chapter 1:

What Suicide Looks Like Beyond The Stereotypes

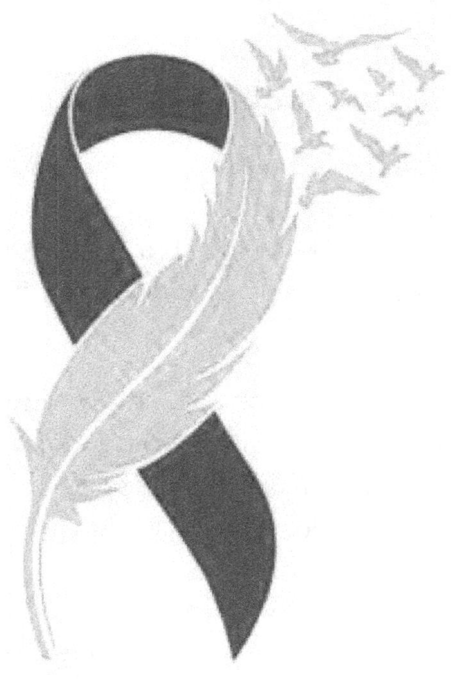

PART I

When most people hear the word suicide, they imagine extremes. They think of dramatic goodbyes, visible breakdowns, open wounds, or someone crying out for help in ways the world can easily see. They picture someone curled in a dark room, or someone with no joy, no friends, no future. They expect warning signs to look loud, chaotic, or obvious. But suicide, in reality, wears many faces, and many of them look nothing like what people imagine.

Sometimes suicide looks like silence.
Sometimes it looks like routine.
Sometimes it looks like laughter.
Sometimes it looks like the strongest one in the room.

The truth is, many people fighting suicidal thoughts are the same ones comforting others, showing up to work, smiling in pictures, posting motivational quotes, and saying "I'm fine" with a steady voice. Not because they are okay, but because hiding feels safer than being misunderstood.

Suicide does not always come as a scream. Often, it arrives quietly, a whisper in the mind, a growing exhaustion in the spirit, a heaviness that builds over time until one day the weight tips. People don't always see it. Sometimes you don't even see it in yourself.

Suicide can look like:

• A woman who laughs loudly but goes home to cry into her pillow
• A teen who makes honor roll yet feels like nothing they do is enough

• A mother who cooks dinner, folds laundry, and silently breaks inside the bathroom

• A man who provides for everyone but has no space to collapse himself

• A friend who is always "the strong one" until strength becomes an invisible cage

• A child who feels unseen, unheard, unwanted, and thinks disappearing is easier than explaining why they hurt.

• A leader who motivates others while battling their own midnight thoughts

It is not always the person withdrawing from the world, sometimes it is the one leading it. The loudest in the room. The helper. The giver. The overachiever. The caretaker. The comedian. The pastor. The teacher. The friend everyone leans on.

It comes in all shapes, forms, and reasons.

People often believe that suicide belongs only to the depressed, the visibly broken, the obviously struggling. But pain is creative, it finds ways to hide. Trauma learns how to blend in. And a wounded soul can still perform life while dying inside.

Suicide does not discriminate. It doesn't ask your age, your income, your beauty, your status, your career, your relationship, or your faith. It can touch anyone, the successful, the struggling, the young, the elderly, the wealthy, the spiritual, the quiet, the strong.

The world has been conditioned to look for the wrong signs, the extreme ones. But more often, suicidal thoughts grow like weeds under the surface, unseen until they choke the life beneath.

I was that hidden struggle.

At thirteen, no one saw my pain. I smiled when required, attended school like normal, existed like every other child. But inside, I was fighting demons with a child's hands. People said I was strong, they had no idea strength was just my survival mechanism. Strength is not always healthy, sometimes it's just a mask.

Suicide, at its core, is not about wanting death. It is often about wanting *relief.*
Relief from unbearable pain.
Relief from shame.
Relief from memories that haunt.
Relief from feeling alone in a room full of people.
Relief from the battle between wanting to live and wanting the suffering to stop.

People don't want to stop their lives; they want to stop the hurting. The more we understand this, the more compassion we build. The more lives we can protect. The more voices we might hear before they fall silent.

If we are going to save lives, we must stop waiting for dramatic signs and start listening for subtle ones, the tired eyes, the forced smiles, the changes in routine, the over-apologizing, the sudden isolation, the giving away of personal items, the random "I love yous," or the calm that comes after a long period of deep sadness. Sometimes calm is not healing, it's surrender.

Suicide is often invisible until it isn't.

And that is why this book begins with truth, the kind that breaks silence, challenges assumptions, and opens our eyes to see what we once overlooked.

Because somewhere right now, someone is smiling, laughing, functioning, surviving, and silently begging for someone to notice the weight they're carrying.

Not everyone wants advice. Some just want to be seen. Some just want someone to ask, "Are you really okay?" and mean it. Some just need one reason to hold on another night.

One reason to wake up tomorrow.

And if this book becomes that reason for even one life, then nothing I survived was in vain.

<u>PART II</u>

The Faces Pain Wears: The Invisible Struggle

Pain rarely introduces itself politely. It slips in quietly, through childhood wounds, heartbreak, loneliness, disappointment, pressure, trauma, silence. It attaches itself to memories we never processed and experiences we were never equipped to handle. Before we realize it, pain is living in us, speaking for us, and sometimes trying to take us from ourselves. People expect pain to look dramatic. But pain is a shapeshifter.

Sometimes it smiles.
Sometimes it gets perfect grades.
Sometimes it goes to work early and stays late.
Sometimes it helps others heal while falling apart alone.

Pain can dress itself in:

- ✓ Confidence
- ✓ Ambition
- ✓ Leadership
- ✓ Humor
- ✓ Beauty
- ✓ Strength

And because of that, many suffer in secret.

WAKE UP TOMORROW

It's not always the person crying out; often, it's the one who believes they aren't allowed to fall apart. The one everyone leans on. The one taught to be strong. The one who never had the space to feel weak.

Pain looks like the mother who never rests because she's afraid if she stops moving, she will fall apart. It looks like the businessman smiling in meetings but drinking himself numb at night. It looks like the student who everyone praises but who whispers prayers into her pillow asking God to take her in her sleep. It looks like the woman who seems put together but stares at herself in the mirror feeling worthless, unseen, unlovable. Pain looks like the "strong friend." And often, no one checks on the strong friend.

We must understand something essential: suicide is not just about death. It is about *escape.*

Escape from memories too heavy to hold.
Escape from expectations too high to reach.
Escape from trauma untreated and misunderstood.
Escape from feeling like you are never enough.
Escape from the war inside your mind.

When hope shrinks, escape looks like peace, and peace, to someone hurting, feels like death might bring it.

This is why understanding matters. This is why compassion matters. This is why presence matters. We cannot save everyone, but we can create fewer silent sufferers.

When we broaden our understanding of what suicidal pain looks like, we stop missing opportunities to intervene. We stop judging people by appearance. We slow down enough to really see each other.

Sometimes the people most at risk are the ones we least suspect.

Suicide does not always look like sadness.
Sometimes it looks like exhaustion.
Sometimes it looks like relief.
Sometimes it looks like silence.
Sometimes it looks like peace that isn't peace, it's surrender.

The enemy of life is not just depression;
it is ***hopelessness.***

The belief that tomorrow offers nothing.
The belief that pain is permanent.
The belief that the world will not miss you.
The belief that no one would understand.

But pain lies.
Depression lies.
Trauma lies.

And this book exists to interrupt those lies.

PART III

How Suicidal Thoughts Grow: The Slow Unseen Decline

Suicidal thoughts rarely arrive as a sudden storm. More often, they drip. Quietly. Slowly. Consistently.

Not always as a loud voice demanding death, sometimes as a whisper suggesting escape. A thought that returns night after night, unnoticed by everyone except the one fighting it.

It begins with pain, emotional, physical, mental, spiritual. Then pain becomes heavy. Heavy becomes exhausting. Exhaustion becomes hopelessness. Hopelessness becomes quiet surrender.

This is the path many walk long before anyone sees the final step. Suicidal thinking often follows a pattern like this:

1. **Hurt**
   Something happens. A trauma. A loss. A betrayal. A violation. A memory that won't fade. A wound that never healed.

2. **Silence**
   You don't talk about it. You don't know how to. You don't want to burden anyone. You fear judgment, disbelief, or blame. So, you swallow it.

3. **Isolation**
   You pull back emotionally, mentally, socially. Not because

you don't want love — but because you don't believe you deserve it or don't know how to receive it.

4. <u>**Numbness**</u>
Feelings fade. Laughter feels forced. Joy feels distant. Days blur. You start existing instead of living.

5. <u>**Hopelessness**</u>
You start believing the situation won't change. That the pain is permanent. That nothing will get better.

6. <u>**Suicidal Ideation**</u>
Not always a plan — sometimes just a thought.
"What if I disappeared?"
"Would anyone notice?"
"Maybe life would be easier without me."

7. <u>**Quite Moments**</u>
It may come during quiet nights, shower thoughts, moments of overwhelm, or while staring at the ceiling wishing for sleep to take everything away.

8. <u>**Suicidal Planning or Attempt**</u>
Not because you want to die, but because you want the pain to stop.

Suicidal thoughts develop in stages and recognizing them early saves lives. This is why *awareness* matters, not just for those struggling, but for families, leaders, teachers, partners, and friends. The earlier we see pain, the more time we have to intervene.

Sometimes the person who needs help doesn't ask because they don't believe they're allowed to. People say things like: "I don't want to bother anyone." "They have their own problems." "It doesn't matter anyway." "They wouldn't understand." Pain convinces us we are burdens, instead of reminding us we are human.

WAKE UP TOMORROW

When suicidal thoughts grow slowly, they become familiar. Familiar pain becomes normal. Normal pain becomes tolerated. Tolerated pain becomes dangerous. And one day, the person who once fought to survive starts being tired of fighting. Not because they are weak, but because they are human.

This chapter is not written to scare, but to open eyes. To encourage early support, early conversations, early intervention. To teach us to check in when someone withdraws, not just when they break.

To look deeper when someone says "I'm okay" too quickly. To watch for subtle changes, not dramatic collapses. To remember that even the strongest need saving sometimes.

You never know whose life you preserve by simply noticing. And if you are the one walking through these stages right now, hear me:

Your pain is real, but so is hope.
Your thoughts are heavy, but they are not permanent.
Your story is wounded but not finished.

You deserve more than survival.
You deserve healing.
You deserve tomorrow.

This book is your reminder of that.

<u>PART IV</u>

When Pain Becomes A Secret

Some wounds bleed silently.

Not every person who is battling suicidal thoughts is loud about their suffering. In fact, many become experts at hiding it. They laugh at the right moments, answer "I'm okay" without hesitation, post pictures that look happy, and move through life like everything is fine.

Because somewhere along the way, pain taught them to hide.

Maybe they tried to speak once and weren't heard.
Maybe they were told to "be strong" or "stop being dramatic."
Maybe their childhood taught them that crying made you weak.
Maybe they were surrounded by people who were too broken to notice their cracks.

When pain isn't validated, it becomes quiet. When pain is quiet too long, it becomes a secret. Secrets start as survival. Then they turn into chains.

We tell ourselves: "I don't want to bother anyone." "No one would understand." "They have bigger problems." "I'm supposed to be the strong one." "If I speak it, it will make it real." And so, we carry it. Alone.

Hidden pain is heavy, but people carry it every day:

- The woman who cooks dinner, laughs with her kids, then cries in the shower so no one hears.
- The man who goes to work like nothing's wrong but drives home with a numb stare.
- The teenager who isolates in their room, scrolling for someone who feels like them.
- The leader who encourages everyone else while silently collapsing inside.

Hiding becomes habit. Pretending becomes normal. Smiles become masks. Strength becomes performance. And the world applauds the performance.

"You're so strong."
"You always seem happy."
"I wish I was as confident as you."
"You handle everything so well."

If only they knew.

People rarely think of checking on the one who looks fine. They do not question the one who's always put together. They look at success, beauty, talent, or status and assume stability. But pain can coexist with achievement. Depression can live inside a beautiful home. Suicidal thoughts can hide inside someone who looks blessed.

Sometimes the saddest people are the best actors. Pain becomes dangerous when we stop believing we're allowed to feel it.

When we force ourselves to "push through," we push down. When we silence our pain, it grows roots. When we hold everything inside, we drown where no one can see.

And if you've ever felt that, if you know what it's like to be smiling in public and praying for peace in private, you are not weak. You are not crazy. You are not alone. You were simply never given space to talk about your hurt.

This chapter is your permission slip to stop carrying secrets that suffocate you. To speak, even shakily. To whisper if you cannot shout. To share your truth with someone safe, even if you've never done it before.

Secrets lose power when spoken. Shame loses grip when exposed to light. Pain begins to heal when it is acknowledged. The girl I was at thirteen had no words for her pain.

No safe place.
No one to tell.
So she held it in, and it almost killed her.

This is why I speak now.
Why I write.
Why this book exists.

Because someone out there is holding secrets heavy enough to break them. Someone is thinking silent thoughts that echo the ones I whispered as a child. Someone is lying in bed tonight saying, "I hope I don't wake up tomorrow."

If that someone is you, lean in:

- You are allowed to tell your story.
- You are allowed to need help.
- You are allowed to fall apart and rebuild.
- You do not have to collapse alone.

WAKE UP TOMORROW

You matter more than your silence.
You matter beyond your pain.
You matter beyond what happened to you.

And you deserve to stay. Not just stay alive, but stay to see healing, peace, joy, fullness. Stay to wake up tomorrow.

Not the quiet kind that brings peace or stillness, but the silence born from swallowed hurt, suppressed emotion, and unspoken pain. The kind of silence that traps trauma inside the body and turns thoughts into heavy stones no one else knows you're carrying. Silence seems like protection at first. A shield. A survival tactic. A way to avoid judgment, shame, or misunderstanding.

But over time, silence becomes a prison.

Every unspoken feeling sits inside the chest like weight.
Every memory you never processed settles in your bones.
Every tear you held back becomes a lump in your throat.
Every scream you swallowed becomes internal noise.

And eventually, silence starts costing things, sometimes everything.

It costs mental peace.
It costs joy.
It costs identity.
It costs connection.
It costs sleep.
It costs self-worth.
It can even cost a life.

Because what we don't speak, we carry. What we carry, we learn to hide. What we hide, we start believing we deserve. Silence teaches you to perform instead of expressing yourself. To function instead of healing. To fake strength instead of feeling pain.

You learn how to:

- Smile when broken.
- Laugh when empty.
- Work while grieving.
- Serve while starving emotionally.
- Love others while hating yourself.

Until one day, you look in the mirror and barely recognize the person staring back. This is the cost of silence.

It slowly disconnects you from your own voice, and without voice, you lose truth. Without truth, you lose grounding. And when you lose grounding, suicidal thoughts find space to grow.

When no one knows your pain, no one knows you need saving. We often think speaking makes us vulnerable, but silence makes us invisible. We think sharing our struggle is weakness, but silence is what weakens us. Pain that has no outlet has only one direction to go, inward.

It buries itself into your identity, whispering lies:

"You're too much."
"You're not enough."
"No one cares."
"You deserve this."
"You should disappear."
And when silence convinces you those lies are true, seeking help feels impossible.

WAKE UP TOMORROW

If you're reading this and silence has been your survival, I want you to know:

You are not wrong for being quiet, you were coping.
You were protecting yourself.
You did what you thought you had to do to survive.

- ✓ But survival is not the end goal, living is.
- ✓ Healing is.
- ✓ Thriving is.
- ✓ Freedom is.

Freedom begins when silence breaks.

You deserve spaces where your truth is welcome.
You deserve people who can hold your story gently.
You deserve to release what has been choking your spirit.
You deserve to speak.

Even if your voice shakes.
Even if you cry through every word.
Even if you don't know where to start.

You can start right here.
Between these pages.
With yourself.

Let this chapter be the first crack in the walls silence built around you. Let this be where your voice begins to awaken. Let this be the moment you whisper, internally or aloud: **I am not okay, and that is allowed.**

There is power in those words.
There is healing in those words.
There is life in those words.

The cost of silence has been high, too high. But now, we begin reclaiming your voice.

One truth at a time.
One feeling at a time.
One tomorrow at a time.

PART V

When Death Feels Like Peace

No one wants to die; they want the pain to stop.

This is one of the hardest truths to explain to people who have never stood in that emotional space. Suicide is rarely about ending life, it's about ending suffering. It is about looking at the weight you carry and believing peace lives on the other side of letting go.

To someone in deep pain, death can begin to masquerade as relief, a quiet place where the noise stops, where the heart finally rests, where the mind is no longer a battlefield. Not because life itself is unwanted, but because *living hurts too much.*

When a person reaches this point, it's not that they lack love, faith, intelligence, or potential, it's that pain has lasted longer than hope. They've fought silently for so long that rest feels like surrender, and surrender feels like release.

When someone says, "I want to die," what they often mean is:

"I'm exhausted."
"I'm overwhelmed."
"I don't know how to continue."
"I feel alone in this."
"I don't see a way out."

When drowning emotionally, death can wrongly appear as the shore. When hopelessness settles in, tomorrow feels like another storm you don't have the energy to survive.

The mind whispers:

"What if peace is on the other side?"
"What if I don't hurt anymore?"
"What if they'll be better off without me?"
"What if this feeling never ends?"

When suicide feels like peace, it's not because someone wants to leave the world, it's because they can't imagine a world where the pain ever ends.

And that is where the danger lives. Because pain lies.

It tells you the storm is forever. It tells you healing is impossible. It tells you you're alone, even when you're not. It tells you no one will care, even though people would break without you. It tells you death is peace, but it never is.

Death doesn't bring peace. It only transfers pain to the people who loved you.

It leaves parents replaying memories wondering what they missed.
It leaves friends shaking, asking themselves why they didn't call.
It leaves children believing your absence was their fault.
It leaves siblings wishing for one more conversation.
It leaves partners shattered, searching for signs they overlooked.
It leaves communities aching quietly, trying to make sense of it all.

WAKE UP TOMORROW

When someone goes, they take their pain but leave a thousand pieces behind. And yet, when your heart is breaking, you don't think about the aftermath, you think about relief.

I know, because I was there.

Thirteen years old, lying in bed with pills in my stomach, asking God not to wake me. I didn't want to disappear from life I wanted to disappear from the pain of living it.

I wanted rest.
I wanted relief.
I wanted peace.

I thought death was peace. I was wrong, but I was hurting too deeply to know it then. Someone reading this right now might feel the same.

If that someone is you, let me speak to you softly:

- ✓ You do not need to die to find peace.
- ✓ You need healing.
- ✓ You need release.
- ✓ You need someone to hear you.
- ✓ You need space to not be okay.
- ✓ You need support, compassion, and time.

Peace is possible in life, not death.

Hope might feel dim today, but hope is like a sunrise even when you can't see it, it's still coming. The darkest nights often come right before morning.

Hold on through the night.
Hold on one more time.
Hold on one more tomorrow.

You do not need to disappear to rest.
You are allowed to seek help and still be strong.
You are allowed to survive and still be exhausted.
You are allowed to heal slowly one sunrise at a time.

You stayed.
You woke up.
You're reading this.
That means something.

It means your story is still unfolding.
It means peace is still possible just not this way.
It means there is more life left in your purpose than you know.

Tomorrow could be the chapter where everything begins to change.
Don't miss what healing might look like.

Stay.
Even if you stay trembling.
Even if you stay confused.
Even if you stay broken.

Stay until peace comes alive.

PART VI

Warning Signs People Often Miss

Suicide is not always announced. It is not always preceded by clear cries for help. Sometimes the warning signs are small, so small that even those closest may not recognize them. But small signs matter.

When someone is considering giving up, the body, the spirit, and the behavior often begin to shift. Not always dramatically, sometimes quietly. Sometimes it is like a slow dimming of light rather than a sudden blackout. Understanding these signs could save a life.

Emotional warning signs:

- Feeling hopeless or saying things like "What's the point?"
- Expressing overwhelming sadness, emptiness, or numbness.
- Saying they feel like a burden to others.
- Increased irritability or emotional outbursts.
- Loss of interest in things they once enjoyed.
- Sudden calm after deep distress (often mistaken as healing).
- A sense of giving up or withdrawing from the future.

Sometimes the most dangerous sign isn't crying, it's silence.

Behavioral warning signs:

- Withdrawing from friends, family, social events
- Sleeping too much or not at all
- Changes in eating habits (overeating or loss of appetite)
- Giving away personal items that hold meaning

- Sudden risky behavior or substance use
- Loss of motivation or responsibilities being neglected
- Talking more about death, escape, or disappearing

"Watch how they fade, not how they fall."

Verbal warning signs.

Sometimes people speak their pain softly, indirectly, or jokingly.

Listen to statements like:

- "I'm tired of this."
- "You'd be better without me."
- "I don't want to be here anymore."
- "I can't do this."
- "I'm not needed."
- "I don't care what happens to me."
- "I wish I could just sleep forever."

Many dismiss these as exaggeration or drama, but they are often **hints of internal war.**

Subtle signs people overlook:

- Sudden interest in personal affairs or unfinished business
- Cleaning or organizing excessively (subconsciously preparing)
- Uncharacteristic generosity
- A drastic change in appearance or personal hygiene
- Turning off their phone, isolating, not replying for long periods
- Avoiding eye contact or deep conversations
- A smile that doesn't reach the eyes

People who are considering suicide don't always look sad, sometimes they look calm, even happy, because they think they've made a final decision. It's important to notice changes, even gentle ones. Behavioral shifts speak louder than words.

A person who was once outgoing became withdrawn. A person who always laughed suddenly losing their spark.
A person who was messy becoming suddenly neat.
A person who always answered calls now letting them ring.

One change alone may not signal danger, but several together could mean someone is silently struggling.

What to do if you notice warning signs

You do not need to have perfect words. You only need to be present. Sometimes a simple conversation can interrupt darkness.

Try:

"I've noticed you haven't been yourself, are you okay?"
"You seem heavy lately talk to me if you want."
"You matter to me. I'm here for you."
"I care about you. You're not alone."

Avoid phrases like:

"Just cheer up."
"You're too strong for this."
"Other people have it worse."
"You're overreacting."

Compassion opens doors, minimizing pain closes them. If someone trusts you with their truth, handle it with care. Your response might be the difference between breaking or healing.

PART VII

Hope As An Interrupt:
One Moment Can Save A Life

Sometimes, all it takes is one interruption.

One phone call.
One text message.
One unexpected laugh.
One memory that surfaces.
One prayer whispered through tears.
One person knocking on the door.
One reason, even a small one, to stay.

When someone is on the edge emotionally, hope does not need to be loud to be effective. Hope just needs to arrive even subtly before the final step.

Hope is often not a miracle moment. It's a flicker. A breath. A pause long enough to reconsider. A voice soft enough to break the silence. A feeling deep enough to say, "Maybe not today."

Hope interrupts despair.

It does not remove the pain instantly. It doesn't erase trauma or magically heal the wounds. But it slows the fall. It creates a gap between thought and action. Sometimes, that tiny space is where life is saved.

For me, the interruption was simple: I woke up. Alive. Sick. Confused. Disappointed but still here.

I didn't recognize it immediately, but waking up was mercy. It was grace. It was God stepping in when I didn't know how to call for Him. It was hope disguised as another morning. Hope doesn't always look like healing. Sometimes hope looks like survival.

Hope is hearing "I love you" unexpectedly.
Hope is remembering you have goals you haven't reached.
Hope is thinking about someone who would miss you.
Hope is imagining your future child or your future self.
Hope is faith whispering, "Hold on, this is not the end."

Hope is the promise of "maybe tomorrow will be softer."

And in dark seasons, **maybe** is powerful.

Sometimes hope comes from people sometimes from within sometimes from God sometimes from pure accident. But however, it arrives, hope matters. It interrupts. It pauses. It creates room for reconsideration, for reaching out, for breathing through one more night. If you are reading this and fighting battles in silence, let this page be your interruption: stay.

Not because everything is perfect but because everything can change. Not because you feel strong but because strength can grow. Not because you don't hurt but because healing is possible.

Your story is still unfolding, and hope can enter your life in ways you don't expect. The moment that changes everything might be closer than you think.

WAKE UP TOMORROW

You may not feel it now, but:

- ✓ There are people you haven't met yet who will love you deeply.
- ✓ There are moments you will laugh again without forcing it.
- ✓ There are places you will stand that you once thought you'd never reach.
- ✓ There are dreams inside you that you haven't touched yet.
- ✓ There is peace ahead of you real peace not the kind pain promises.

Hope is not a fantasy. Hope is a lifeline. Keep waking up tomorrow.

Even if you must climb out of bed slowly.
Even if your thoughts are heavy.
Even if you don't know how to keep going.
Even if all you can say is "not today."

That is enough.
You are enough.

You're not expected to heal overnight.
Just stay alive long enough to see what healing looks like.

<u>PART VIII</u>

What Keeps Us Alive Reasons To Stay

People often ask:
"What stops someone from going through with suicide?"
"What makes a person stay just one more day?"
For many, the answer isn't one big reason it's a collection of small ones.

A moment.
A memory.
A heartbeat.
A whisper of faith.
A face.
A dream.
A future they haven't met yet.

Sometimes the reason is as simple as:

"I don't want to hurt my family."
"I want to see my child grow up."
"I want to graduate."
"I don't want to leave my pets."
"I promised someone I'd show up tomorrow."

Sometimes it's even quieter:

"I'm curious what next year might look like."
"What if things get better?"
"What if I laugh again?"

Even the faintest spark can hold someone to life. Hope doesn't need to roar it just needs to exist. Purpose doesn't need to be clear only possible.

People stay for so many reasons:

- A child who still needs them
- A dream that hasn't lived yet
- A prayer not yet answered
- A future version of themselves they want to meet
- The possibility of healing
- Love even if they can't feel it yet
- Faith even when shaken
- The desire to try one more time

Sometimes people stay because someone noticed. Because someone checked in. Because someone said "I love you" at the right moment. Because someone saw through their smile and asked again. And sometimes they stay because, deep down, some part of them still wants to live, even if another part wants to disappear.

It is okay to feel torn. It is okay to want relief and want life at the same time. Both can be true. Staying alive doesn't mean you are healed, it means you haven't given up on healing.

Staying is brave.

You may not see your strength, but every breath you take is an act of courage. Every sunrise you wake to is a step forward. You are surviving something that once tried to take you, that means something powerful lives inside you.

Think about this: There are people you haven't met yet who will love you with a softness you've never known. There are opportunities on the way you can't imagine from where you stand now. There is peace ahead of you that will feel like breathing after years underwater. There is a healed version of you who will look back and thank you for staying.

Hold on for **them**. Hold on for **you**. Hold on for **tomorrow**. Because reasons to die are loud in the moment, but reasons to live last much longer.

Sometimes the question isn't: "Why stay alive?"

Sometimes it's: "What do I want to live long enough to see?"

A new chapter. A healed heart. A baby is born into your arms. A book written. A business launched. A love that feels safe. A peace that finally holds you. A future where you don't hurt like this anymore.

It might feel distant, but it is real.
It might feel impossible, but it is waiting.
It might take time, but you are worth time.

You deserve to see what's on the other side of this pain.

Stay. For love. For purpose. For healing. For one more chance. For one more sunrise.

Stay for the life you haven't lived yet.

PART IX

Inside the Mind Of Someone
Who Just Wants Peace

There is a misconception that people who think about suicide want to die. But most don't.

They want **relief**.
They want **quiet**.
They want **rest** from the storm.
They want **the pain to stop**, not life itself.

To understand suicidal thoughts, we must step inside that internal world, not as strangers, but as witnesses. We must see what the person sees, feel what they feel, hear what their mind whispers when the lights go out and the room falls silent. Inside the mind of someone struggling, life doesn't end in one loud moment, it unravels slowly.

Thoughts deepen like water. Emotions pile like weight. Hope slips like sand through fingers.

And the brain begins to tell stories that pain wrote:
"No one would miss me."
"I'm tired of trying."
"Maybe peace is on the other side of letting go."
"This hurt feels permanent."
Not dramatic: numb.

Not loud: quiet.
Not impulsive: exhausted.

It's the kind of tired sleep doesn't fix. Everyday tasks start feeling like mountains: Getting out of bed requires strength that no one sees. Showering feels like effort. Answering the phone feels impossible. Smiling feels like lying. Breathing feels like work.

Thoughts become heavy, repetitive, consuming:

"What if I wasn't here?"
"What if I disappeared?"
"What if I could just rest?"

Not always prompted by tragedy, sometimes prompted by accumulation.

Trauma layered on trauma.
Loss on top of loss.
Disappointment stacked on disappointment.

Until the mind begins to believe:

"Maybe life isn't for me."
"Maybe everyone would be better if I was gone."
"Maybe ending is easier than fighting."

These thoughts aren't chosen; they evolve through loneliness, shame, exhaustion, and pain. Inside this mental space, the person is not thinking about death as destruction, but as *relief.*

A release. A quiet room. A place without noise. Without memories. Without pressure. Without expectations. Without heartache.

WAKE UP TOMORROW

Pain becomes so loud that silence looks like peace. But suicidal thinking is not a desire for death, it is a desire for life without suffering. There is a version of them who still wants to live.

A small voice, sometimes faint, but always present, yet whispering:
"Maybe stay."
"Maybe there's more."
"Maybe one more day."

The goal of intervention isn't to convince them that pain isn't real. It's to remind them that pain isn't permanent. That there is life beyond this moment. That peace is possible in living, not dying. That tomorrow might hold something their pain cannot imagine today.

Inside the mind of someone who wants peace, there is conflict: two voices, battling softly. One says, "I'm tired. I want this to stop." The other says, "I don't really want to die. I just don't know how to live like this."

This chapter is for that war. For the space between despair and desire to stay. For the tension between exhaustion and hope. It is in that space we can intervene, understand, support, and change outcomes. Because when someone feels seen, understood, and not alone in their thoughts, the mind shifts, even slightly, toward staying.

Toward trying one more time.
Toward waking up tomorrow.
Toward choosing life again.

Not because the pain disappears,
but because connection reminds the heart it is worth healing.

"Though no one can go back and make a brand-new start, anyone can start and make a brand new ending."

- Carl Bard

Chapter 2:

The Battle Between Wanting To Live & Wanting To Escape

<u>PART I</u>

No one teaches us about the war that happens in the quiet. The kind fought not with weapons, but with thoughts. Not against others, but within the self. A war where both sides want something completely different, yet both sides are driven by pain.

One side wants to live. The other side wants to escape. The conflict feels like being pulled in two directions at once: "I want to be here... but I don't know how much more I can take." "I want to live my life... but I'm tired of fighting every day." "I want to stay...but I want the pain to stop."

This battle is invisible from the outside. People see the smile, the functioning, the routine, but they don't see the internal tug-of-war. They don't see the nights where you sit in the dark, staring at the wall or the ceiling, thinking questioning negotiating with yourself just to make it to morning.

They don't see the moments when you stand in the bathroom mirror looking at your reflection like a stranger, whispering inside, "I don't want to die, but I don't want to live like this."

This is where suicidal thoughts often arise. Not from a desire to end life, but from a desperate desire to end the suffering. The mind begins to argue:

"What if leaving is easier than hurting?"
vs. "What if tomorrow is better than today?"

"What if no one notices if I go?" vs. "What if someone would break without me?"

"What if I have nothing left?" vs. "What if I'm closer to healing than I realize?"

Some nights, escape feels stronger. Other days, life feels possible. And most days, it's both. Living while hurting is like trying to walk on broken legs.

Possible, but painful.
Exhausting.
Slow.

But healing is like physical therapy for the soul, not immediate, but gradual. Not painless, but worth it.

In this battle, small things become anchors:

A child's laugh.
A future dream.
A moment of joy.
A voice that checks in.
A prayer whispered shakily.
A sunrise after a night you didn't think you'd survive.

These are tiny victories, but they matter. Because every time you choose to stay, even if only for one more hour, one more sunrise, one more tomorrow, life wins.

It may not feel like victory.
It may feel like crawling.
It may feel like surviving by a thread.

But survival is still survival and staying is still choosing life. And every time you stay, you give yourself another chance at the life your pain told you you'd never reach. There is a future version of you who is grateful you held on.

Who has peace instead of pain.
Who has joy instead of numbness.
Who is living instead of battling to exist.

You are fighting for them, and they are worth the fight. This chapter is not about glamorizing the struggle but acknowledging it honestly. You are not weak for wanting to escape. You are not wrong for feeling torn. You are not broken because part of you wants out.

You are human. You are hurting. And you are trying.

Trying is courageous.
Staying is powerful.
Healing is possible.

You can want to live and want to rest at the same time. You can desire peace without wanting death. You don't have to choose between living in pain or dying, there is a third path: **healing**. And healing is slow, but real. Soft, but strong. Fragile, but transforming.

You are not weak for fighting; you are brave in continuing the battle. One day, escape will no longer look like relief. Peace will not be tied to death. Tomorrow will not feel heavy, it will feel hopeful.

Hold on until that day arrives.
Stay until peace meets you alive.

Chapter 3:

The Cry for Help We Don't Hear

<u>PART I</u>

Not every cry for help sounds like a scream. Sometimes it sounds like a whisper. Sometimes it looks like isolation. Sometimes it feels like distance. Sometimes it hides inside humor, sarcasm, or silence.

People imagine cries for help as dramatic breakdowns, sobbing confessions, or desperate phone calls, but in reality, many cries for help are subtle, misunderstood, or easily overlooked.

Sometimes the most heartbreaking plea is not:
"I want to die,"
but rather, "I'm tired,"
"I can't do this anymore,"
"I don't feel like myself,"
or even, "I'm fine."
The world hears words, but pain speaks in behavior.

Sometimes crying for help looks like:

- Pushing everyone away.
- Answering texts less.
- Cancelling plans without explanation.
- Taking longer to respond, or not at all.
- Sitting in the car before going inside.
- Sleeping excessively or barely sleeping.
- Starting arguments or becoming easily irritated.
- Giving hints but never saying it directly.

Some people cry for help by changing how they show up. Others cry for help by not showing up at all. We must learn to listen differently. The cry for help is often not the dramatic moment, it's the weeks, months, or years leading up to it. The small comments brushed off. The decline in energy. The smile fading but still present enough to fool the room. Many times, people want help but don't know how to ask for it.

Why?

Because asking feels risky.
Vulnerable.
Shameful.
Like exposing a wound no one else will know how to hold.

They fear being called dramatic. Fear hearing "pray about it" with no support. Fear being misunderstood or minimized. Fear of burdening others. Fear looking ungrateful or weak.

So instead of saying: "I need help," they say, "Don't worry about me." Instead of saying: "I'm drowning," they say, "I'm just tired." Instead of saying: "I want to disappear," they laugh and make a joke about it.

We live in a world that is more connected than ever, yet people feel more alone than they've ever been. With social media, curated images, and highlight reels, pain is easy to hide behind filters.

Someone can post smiling photos while planning their last day. Someone can share motivation while battling thoughts at midnight. Someone can inspire others while losing themselves inside. This is why compassion must be proactive—not reactive.

Instead of waiting for someone to collapse before caring, check in when they grow quiet. Ask again when they say "I'm fine" too quickly. Notice when their energy changes. Pay attention to the shift, not just the words.

People need space to speak without fear, to hurt without shame, to admit they're not okay without feeling weak. Sometimes, the most powerful thing you can say to someone is: "I see you. You don't have to carry this alone. Talk to me if you want—no judgment, just presence."

Many lives could be saved with one conversation, one safe moment, one person willing to see past the surface. Sometimes help doesn't require answers, just listening. Just sitting with them. Just being present in pain. Because silence with support is better than words with dismissal.

Let this chapter teach us to hear pain differently. Not through noise, but through absence. Not only through tears, but through the lack of them. Not only through what is said, but what is not said. And if **you** are the one crying quietly, hoping someone might notice, let this be your confirmation:

Your voice matters.
Your feelings are valid.
Your pain is real.
You deserve support.

Even when the world seems loud, your whisper deserves to be heard. You do not have to wait until life breaks open to ask for help.

You can ask now.
You can speak now.
You can choose tomorrow now.

This chapter is the beginning of breaking silence, so cries for help no longer go unheard.

PART II

Storm Behind The Smile:
The Strong Friends & Hidden Pain

We all know someone who seems unbreakable.

The one who shows up for everyone.
The one people call when they need advice.
The one who lifts others, prays for others, comforts others.
The one who laughs loudest, works hardest, carries the weight of the world quietly.

The strong friend.

Society praises strength. But strength often hides suffering. Because when you're always the strong one, people forget to ask if you're okay.

Strong doesn't mean unhurt. Success doesn't mean stable. Smiling doesn't mean healed. Quiet doesn't mean peace. Sometimes the strongest people are the most fragile inside, not because they are weak, but because they carry weight for everyone else while holding their own pain in silence.

The strong friend says things like:
"I got it."
"I'll handle it."
"I'm okay."
"Don't worry about me."
And everyone believes them.

But what they often mean is:
"I don't know how to fall apart."
"No one checks on me."
"I don't feel allowed to need help."
"I'm tired of being strong."
The storm behind the smile is real.

You can be a light for others while sitting in your own darkness. You can lead, love, uplift, and still feel empty at night. You can encourage others to stay, while fighting to stay yourself. Being strong for everyone can make you invisible when you need help.

People forget to check on the one who never asks. They assume you're okay because you always are. They rely on you so much that they don't notice when your hands are shaking.

When your smile becomes a mask. When your strength becomes prison, and the strong friend starts saying:

"I'm tired."
"I need a break."
"I wish someone would see me."

But rarely out loud. Because being the strong one becomes identity. And identity becomes responsibility. And responsibility becomes isolation.

So many strong women, men, mothers, leaders, and survivors are carrying silent storms, holding back tears because they believe breaking makes them a burden. But strength isn't the absence of pain, it's surviving despite it.

WAKE UP TOMORROW

Even warriors lay down their armor to rest.
Even healers need healing.
Even the strong need someone to say:

"You don't have to hold this alone."

If you are the strong friend reading this:

You are allowed to need help. You are allowed to collapse sometimes. You are allowed to cry, scream, rest, step back, breathe. You are not built to carry everyone forever. You deserve support as deeply as you give it. Strength is never breaking. Real strength is knowing when to reach for a hand.

And if you love a strong friend, check on them. Don't wait for them to ask, they probably won't. Send a message. Stop by. Ask twice, not once. Pay attention to the tone behind "I'm okay." Sometimes the strongest are the closest to the edge because no one thinks they are.

Don't let the smile fool you.
Don't let the success blind you.
Don't let the strength silence them.

Look deeper.
Listen softer.
Love harder.

A check-in could save a life.
A conversation could interrupt despair.
A hug could break years of held-back tears.

Sometimes all a strong friend needs is for someone to notice they're human too.

<u>PART III</u>

The Codes People Speak in When They Want Help but Don't Ask Directly

People rarely say, "I'm thinking of ending my life."

Instead, they speak in softer language.
Indirect language.
Language wrapped in protection, fear, or shame.

They hint.
They test the waters.

They hope someone hears what they *didn't* say out loud. Because saying, "I want to die" feels too naked. Too risky. Too final. So the message becomes coded, hidden inside everyday words.

Here are some things people say that truly mean, **"I'm not okay."**

The Tired Code

- ✓ "I'm tired."
- ✓ "I'm exhausted."
- ✓ "I just don't have anything left."

They don't mean physically tired, they mean *emotionally drained*. Life-tired. Fight-tired.

The Disappearing Code

- "Maybe I should just leave."
- "I don't think I belong here."
- "Everyone would be fine without me."

These are not dramatic statements; they're *testing whether they matter.*

The Peace Code

- "I just want it all to be quiet."
- "I wish I could sleep forever."
- "I just want peace."

Not peace from a long day, peace from pain.

The Humor Code

- "If I disappear, don't look for me."
- "I'm one bad day away from losing it."
- Jokes about death, ending it all, or "checking out."

People laugh, but sometimes humor hides the truth.

The Ending Code

- "I'm done."
- "I don't care anymore."
- "What's the point?"

These phrases signal *emptiness,* not laziness. Hopelessness, not apathy.

The Goodbye Code

- Random "I love you" messages
- Giving away personal belongings
- Bringing closure to past conflicts

People sometimes say goodbye without saying goodbye.

The Calm Code

A sudden calm after chaos. A peaceful tone after weeks of distress.

This is the most misunderstood sign of all. People think, "They're finally better." But sometimes, they've simply made a decision.

These codes matter. If we learn to hear them, we can intervene earlier. A conversation could interrupt the plan. A question could break the silence. A moment of presence could save a life.

Because underneath coded language is a deeper message:
"I need someone to see me."
"I'm drowning and scared to say it plainly."
"I don't want to bother anyone."
"I want someone to notice without me having to shout."

And the truth: "I want to stay, but I don't know how."

If you have ever spoken in codes...
even without knowing... you are not strange or dramatic.
You were communicating the only way you knew how.

And if someone you love uses these phrases, lean in.

Ask gently.
Listen deeply.
Show presence instead of pressure.

WAKE UP TOMORROW

Try asking:

"What does 'tired' really mean for you?"
"When you say you don't care, what do you feel inside?"
"I heard what you said, but how are you, really?"

Curiosity is a form of love.
Listening is a form of rescue.

Sometimes just feeling understood is enough to pull someone back from the edge.

<u>PART IV</u>

When No One Hears The Cry
(The Pain Of Feeling Unseen)

There is a special kind of heartbreak that comes from calling out silently and hearing nothing back. Not the heartbreak of losing a relationship, but the heartbreak of losing belief that someone could care enough to notice.

When you hint at pain, even subtly, and the world keeps moving as if nothing has changed, you learn to shrink.

You learn to swallow feelings whole. To water down your pain so it doesn't spill onto anyone else. You learn to smile wider, laugh harder, pretend better, because it hurts to be unseen.

Unheard.
Misunderstood.
Overlooked.
Invisible.

- ✓ Sometimes the cry for help is so soft even the person crying barely hears it.
- ✓ Sometimes pain becomes so normal you forget what peace feels like.
- ✓ Sometimes you convince yourself you don't deserve to be saved.

And when the world doesn't look closely, you begin to believe your presence, and absence would both go un-noticed.

WAKE UP TOMORROW

This is where hopelessness grows. When someone says, "No one would care if I was gone," that is not a dramatic statement. That is despair speaking, it is a confession of invisibility.

Because the deepest desire for a hurting soul does not escape, but to be seen, held, understood. To know that someone would notice if they disappeared.

When cries for help go unheard, the mind tells dangerous lies:
"You don't matter."
"You're replaceable."
"You're too much."
"You're alone in this."
"No one will come even if you scream."
And lies, when repeated internally long enough, begin to sound like truth.

But here is the truth pain tries to hide:
You are not invisible.
You are not too much.
You are not replaceable.
You are not unworthy of care.
Your existence matters more than you know.
Even if no one fought for you before, that does not mean no one will fight for you now. Even if your childhood taught you silence, your adulthood can teach you voice. Even if someone missed your cry in the past, someone else can hear it today.

Do not swallow your scream.
Do not apologize for needing help.
Do not calm your pain to make others comfortable.

Healing begins where honesty meets compassion. And even if your cry was unheard before, let this book hear it. Let this page hold it. Let this moment recognize it.

You are seen here.
You are heard here.
You matter here.

Your story is not too heavy.
Your heart is not too late.
Your life is not beyond restoration.

Sometimes help doesn't come when you whisper, but it doesn't mean you weren't worth hearing. It means you needed a louder voice. A safer space. A listener who understands the language of pain. This is that space.

Speak.
Write.
Cry.
Pour the truth out of your ribs.
Break the silence that once broke you.

Pain thrives in darkness, but it dies in light.

This chapter is the light.

PART V

How to Respond When Someone Shows Signs, They're Not Okay

When someone is hurting, your response matters more than you may ever realize. A calm voice can interrupt chaos. A gentle question can open a locked heart. A moment of presence can save a life.

You do not need a degree in counseling.
You do not need perfect words.
You do not need to fix everything.

You just need to care — and show it.

When you sense something is off, say something. Silence can feel like abandonment to a struggling soul. Checking in might feel small to you, but it could be lifesaving to them. Start with noticing.

Pay attention if:
- They withdraw or isolate
- They stop showing up
- Their energy feels different
- They've been "too quiet lately"
- Their personality shifts
- They speak in codes or hopeless language

Pay attention to *changes*, not just behaviors.

<u>Step 1</u>: Ask, and ask again

Many hurting people will answer automatically: "I'm fine." "I'm okay." Not because they're okay, but because they're used to hiding. So, ask again, gently.

Try:

- "You seem different lately. Are you really okay?"
- "I noticed you've been quieter — talk to me if you want."
- "I care about you, and I'm here to listen. What's going on?"

Sometimes the second question opens the truth.

Step 2: Listen without fixing

When someone opens up, don't rush to solve.
Don't minimize.
Don't spiritualize away pain.
Don't dismiss or compare.

Just *listen*.

Let them talk.
Let them cry.
Let them unload.
Let silence sit if needed.

Your presence is more important than perfect speech.

Instead of:

"It could be worse."
"You'll get over it."
"You're strong, you'll be fine."
"Other people have bigger problems."

Try:

"That sounds heavy, thank you for trusting me."
"You're not alone. I'm here with you."
"I'm glad you told me. How can I support you right now?"
"It's okay to feel this. You don't have to hide it."

Validation heals more than advice.

Step 3: Ask direct but gentle questions

Many fear asking directly about suicide, but clarity can save a life.

Try:

"Have you had thoughts about wanting to disappear?"
"Do you sometimes feel like you don't want to be here?"
"Have you thought about hurting yourself?"

Asking won't put the idea in their mind. But not asking may leave them alone with it.

Step 4: Don't leave them alone in dark moments

If someone admits they're suicidal:

• Stay with them
• Remove access to means if possible
• Contact support, do not handle it alone
• Call a hotline or crisis resource together
• In emergencies, call for professional help

Their life is more important than discomfort.

Step 5: Follow up later

Support isn't a one-time conversation.
Check in tomorrow.
And the next day.
And randomly when they don't expect it.

Not to nag, but to remind them they matter continuously.

Send messages like:

- "Thinking of you today."
- "How is your heart?"
- "You crossed my mind, you are important to me."

Consistency builds safety.
Safety builds trust.
Trust opens doors for healing.

Remember:

You don't have to be the savior.
You just must be human.

Show up.
Ask.
Listen.
Stay.
Follow through.

Even small care can feel like light to someone sitting in darkness.

PART VI

Why People Don't Ask For Help

It is easy from the outside to wonder:

"Why didn't they just say something?"
"Why didn't they call?"
"Why didn't they tell anyone they were struggling?"

But when you are the one inside the pain, the answer is never simple. People don't ask for help not because they don't need it — but because something inside them has convinced them that they shouldn't, or that they can't.

1. Fear of judgment

Many fears being labeled:

- ✓ Weak.
- ✓ Crazy.
- ✓ Dramatic.
- ✓ Unstable.
- ✓ Broken.

They worry about whispers, gossip, or misunderstanding.
They fear being looked at differently tomorrow.

2. Belief that no one will understand

Pain can isolate the mind. It says:

"No one gets you."
"They'll think you're overreacting."
"You'll have to explain everything, and you don't have the energy."

So, silence feels easier, even when it hurts more.

3. Not wanting to be a burden

People who hurt deeply often care deeply.
They don't want to add weight to anyone else's life.

"I don't want to stress anyone."
"They have their own problems."
"I don't want to be too much."

So, they become caretakers instead of care receivers.

4. Independence and pride

Especially those who are used to surviving alone.
Those who had to grow up fast.
Those who have always been "the strong one."

"I should handle this myself."
"I don't want help, I'm used to doing it alone."

But strength without support becomes suffocation.

5. Childhood messaging

Some were taught:

"Stop crying."
"Be strong."

"You're fine."
"Keep it to yourself."

So they learned early that feelings weren't welcome.

6. Cultural silence

In many families and communities:

Therapy is shameful.
Mental health is "weakness."
Suicide is taboo.
Pain is denied or minimized.

We tell people to pray it away, but prayer and help can coexist.

7. They don't know what help looks like

How do you ask for something you've never received?
How do you speak pain when you've only ever swallowed it?
How do you reach for comfort you've never tasted?

Some people know how to survive, but not how to be supported.

8. They think help won't change anything

Hopelessness dulls vision.
It says:

"This is just who I am."
"Nothing will get better."
"What's the point?"

When hope shrinks, help feels pointless, even though it's not.

9. They're afraid of the truth coming out

Asking for help means opening wounds.
Opening wounds means feeling them.
Feeling them means facing them.

And some pain is so deep that facing it feels like dying in itself.

10. They don't think they deserve help

One of the cruelest effects of trauma is shame.
Shame tells you you're unworthy of love, healing, care, or life.

"They'd be better without me."
"I'm the problem."
"I don't deserve support."

But these are lies pain teaches, not truths.

People don't ask for help because pain rewires their thinking.
It silences them.
It isolates them.
It convinces them that speaking will make things worse.

But the truth is:

Asking for help is not weakness, it's courage. Reaching out is not burdening, it's survival. Speaking up is not selfish, it's necessary.

You deserve support. You deserve healing. You deserve to be heard. You deserve to stay alive. If no one told you that before, let these words be your permission:

It is okay to need help.
It is okay to ask for help.

WAKE UP TOMORROW

It is okay to not be okay.
It is okay to want to live even when life hurts.

You are not weak for struggling, you are strong for still being here.

PART VII

Barriers To Reaching Out:
Shame, Fear, Pride, Culture, Faith

Reaching out sounds simple, until you are the one hurting.

From the outside, it seems logical to say, "Just tell someone how you feel." But inside pain, vulnerability feels like exposure. And exposure feels like danger. People don't always stay silent because they want to, many stay silent because something stands in the way.

1. Shame

Shame says:

"You shouldn't feel this way."
"You're broken."
"You're the problem."

Shame convinces you that your pain is proof of failure.
It turns suffering into self-blame.
It makes asking for help feel embarrassing or undeserved.

Shame isolates.

2. Fear

Fear asks:

"What if they judge me?"
"What if they leave?"

"What if they don't believe me?"
"What if I make things worse?"

Fear imagines rejection before it even happens. Fear makes silence feel safer than honesty, even when silence hurts more.

3. Pride

Pride whispers: "I don't need anyone." "I can handle this alone." "I'm used to surviving by myself."

For those who had to be strong growing up, asking for help feels like weakness, even when it's courage. Pride is not arrogance, it's self-protection. A shield built from years of holding everything alone.

4. Cultural Conditioning

Some of us come from homes where feelings were not safe. Where crying meant disrespect. Where vulnerability was punished. Where strength meant silence.

We were taught to endure, not express. To cope, not heal. To "get over it," not talk about it. In some communities, mental health is taboo. Therapy is frowned upon. Suicide is denied or misinterpreted as lack of faith. So, pain becomes a family secret.

5. Faith-Based Misunderstandings

Faith is powerful, but faith without understanding can become pressure.

Too many are told:

"Pray harder."
"You're under spiritual attack."

"You need more faith." "God won't give you more than you can bear." So, people feel guilty for struggling.

But hear this:
You can fight spiritually **and** seek professional help.
You can believe in God **and** need therapy.
You can pray **and** cry out to someone you trust.
Healing is not either/or, it is both/and.

God uses people, therapy, medicine, and community as tools of rescue. Asking for help doesn't mean you lack faith, it means you are using what God provided.

6. The "Strong Black Woman/Man" Narrative

(If culturally relevant, this remains powerful)

Many of us were raised to be unbreakable.
To hold the family.
To be the anchor.
To never fall apart.

"Be strong."
"Don't let them see you cry."
"We don't talk about that."

Strength became armor, but also prison. The strong one learns to carry everyone, but never themselves.

7. Fear of Being a Burden

This may be the most universal barrier.

People think:

"They have their own problems."
"I don't want to bother anyone."
"They won't want to hear all this."

But needing help does not make you a burden. Sharing your struggle is not dumping, it's release. You are not "too much" you are human.

8. Not Knowing How to Ask

Some have spent so long surviving silently that they don't know how to speak pain. "How do I tell someone I'm drowning?" "How do I explain something I barely understand?"

So, they hope someone will notice without needing to ask. But often, no one sees what is not shown. These barriers do not make you weak. They make you human, shaped by life, culture, pain, expectations, and environment.

But barriers can be broken.
Slowly.
Gently.
Bravely.

Speaking your truth is not betrayal to your culture. Asking for help is not weakness to your faith. Letting others hold you is not abandoning pride; it is allowing love.

You don't have to choose between strength and vulnerability. You can be both.

You can be strong in public and heal in private. Strong in spirit and soft in heart. Strong enough to stay, and strong enough to ask for support.

Freedom begins when barriers fall.
Healing begins when silence lifts.
Life begins again when you believe you are worthy of help.

You are worthy.

Not later.
Not when you "have it together."
Not when you feel healed.

Now.
As you are.
In your pain.
In your process.

You deserve help.
You deserve healing.
You deserve tomorrow.

PART VIII

The Power Of One Safe Person

Sometimes healing doesn't begin with a therapist, a clinic, a program, or a plan. Sometimes it begins with just *one* safe person. One person who listens without judging. One person who notices without being told. One person who doesn't try to fix you, just sits with you in the hurt.

You don't need a crowd.
You don't need everyone to understand.
You just need *someone.*

A safe person is not perfect; they are present. They don't need answers, they offer space. They don't silence you, they make room for your voice.

A safe person says:
"What you feel is real."
"You're not crazy."
"You don't have to hide with me."
"I'm here, even if you don't have the words yet."
And slowly, walls begin to lower.
Breathing becomes lighter.
Relief becomes possible.
Hope returns, even if softly.

Because presence is medicine too.

What does a safe person feel like?

• Someone you can cry in front of without apology
• Someone who listens to understand, not respond
• Someone you trust with your pain
• Someone who stays consistent, even when you struggle
• Someone who doesn't shame you for how you cope
• Someone who sees you beyond your strength
• Someone who remembers to check in, not only when you're smiling

With the right person, you don't feel like too much. You feel like human, allowed, accepted, held. For many, the fear of opening up is not fear of speaking, but fear of being mishandled. A safe person handles hearts with care. One person can be the difference between giving up and holding on.

History has shown it.
Stories have testified it.
People alive today can confirm it.

Sometimes the text that says, *"Are you home?"* saves someone from a dark decision. Sometimes the phone call that says, *"Just checking on you"* interrupts despair. Sometimes a hug breaks a wall silence built for years. Sometimes a person stays alive because someone else sees them, truly sees them, when they are fading. That is the power of one safe person.

They don't need to understand everything, just be willing to walk beside you while you figure it out. Healing is not always about solutions. Often, it is about connection.

WAKE UP TOMORROW

Connection reminds the brain that it is not alone.
Connection reminds the heart that it matters.
Connection reminds the soul that tomorrow is worth trying for.

And for someone drowning, one hand in the water can feel like salvation. If you have ever been that safe person for someone, thank you. You may not realize it, but your presence could have saved a life.

If you have wished for that safe person and never had one, let this book stand in the gap until they arrive.

You deserve relationships where your truth is welcome.
You deserve friends who check in without being asked.
You deserve a love that holds you through the night.
You deserve support that doesn't disappear when you struggle.
You deserve to be safe somewhere.

And if you haven't found that person yet, hear this: There are people in the world capable of loving you gently. There are souls aligned with your healing. There are hearts waiting to meet you. Your safe person may not be in your life yet, but they exist.

Stay long enough to find them.
Stay long enough to become one for yourself.
Stay long enough to see that life holds community beyond pain.

Your story is not meant to be walked alone.

PART IX

The Weight Of "Be Strong"
(Strength Culture & Toxic Resilience)

"Be strong."

Two words that sound empowering but often feel like chains. From childhood to adulthood, many of us were raised on resilience like it was oxygen. We were taught to endure instead of expressing ourselves. To survive instead of healing. To wipe tears instead of question why they fell.

Strength became identity.
Strength became duty.
Strength became armor.
Strength became silence.

But the truth nobody told us is this: constant strength is exhausting.

You cannot carry a thousand emotional pounds forever without breaking somewhere, internally or externally. And yet, society praises the strong while overlooking the cost of staying that way.

Being strong can mean holding everyone's weight but never releasing your own. Putting your needs last because everyone needs you first. Smiling when you want to scream. Fighting battles no one sees. Being dependable even when you're depleted. Strength becomes a performance, and performances become prisons.

People admire the strong one, but rarely ask: "Who holds you?" "What do *you* need?" "What happens when the strong one gets tired?"

The world claps for your strength, but strength without support is self-destruction disguised as resilience.

Being strong should not mean:

- You never cry
- You never break
- You never need help
- You handle everything alone
- You swallow emotions in silence

True strength is not hiding pain, it's surviving through it with honesty and heart. Yet many of us learned early that vulnerability is danger: "Toughen up." "Don't show weakness." "Stop crying before I give you something to cry about." "Handle it." So, strength became a shield we never put down.

But shields get heavy. Armor rusts. Even warriors collapse when no one offers rest.

The weight of "be strong" eventually becomes: "I must not break." "I must not ask for help." "I must carry everything alone." Until strength begins to feel like suffocation.

There is a difference between: *Strength that protects you* and Strength that isolates you.

Strength without softness becomes numbness. Strength without expression becomes depression. Strength without rest becomes burnout. Strength without connection becomes despair.

You can be strong and still struggle.
You can be strong and still cry.
You can be strong and still ask for help.
You can be strong and still need someone to hold your hand through the night.

Strength and vulnerability are not enemies; they are twins.
Both necessary.
Both human.
Both are sacred.

Your strength does not disappear when you break, it becomes more honest. Healing lives in the space where strength meets softness. When you allow yourself to rest, to release, to feel, you are not weakening. You are freeing yourself from the weight of pretending.

There is power in saying: "I'm tired." "I need support." "I can't do this alone anymore." "Please help me." Those words do not diminish your strength; they prove it.

The strongest people are not the ones who never fall. They are the ones who rise again, ask for support when needed, and choose to keep waking up tomorrow.

You do not always have to be the rock.
You are allowed to be held.
You are allowed to breathe.
You are allowed to exhale your pain.

Sometimes the bravest thing you can do is put the armor down.

<u>PART X</u>

When Strength Becomes Survival Mode (Functioning But Not Living)

There comes a point where strength is no longer empowerment, it becomes survival. You wake up, but you don't feel awake. You move through the day, but you don't feel present. You smile, but your eyes don't glow. You breathe, but it feels like you're only inhaling pain and exhaling exhaustion. You're functioning but not living.

Survival mode is a place many people live in for months, years, or even decades without recognizing it. It becomes routine. A silent autopilot. A life held together by obligation rather than joy.

You continue because you must. Because people depend on you. Because life won't pause for your pain. Because bills need paying, children need feeding, duties need fulfilling.

So, you keep pushing.
Keep smiling.
Keep showing up.
Keep holding strong.

Until strength stops feeling powerful,
and begins to feel like pressure.

Survival mode whispers: "Just get through the day." "Don't break now." "You can cry later." "No one needs to know." Survival mode makes suffering look normal.

You work.
You parent.
You clean.
You laugh occasionally.
You post on social media.
You say you're tired, but no one hears the truth behind those words.

Because survival looks functional. Pain looks productive. Silence looks stable and strength looks admirable. Let's be honest, the world applauds you for enduring what is quietly breaking you. But survival is not the same as living.

Living is waking up with purpose.
Feeling joy without guilt.
Laughing from the soul, not the throat.
Breathing without heaviness.
Resting without fear.
Existing without pretending.

Living is freedom, and many of us have forgotten what that feels like.

When strength becomes survival mode, you may notice:

- You feel numb or disconnected
- You stop dreaming about the future
- You lose passion for things you used to love
- You feel heavy without knowing why
- Joy feels foreign, like it belongs to someone else
- You're always tired — even after sleep
- You go through motions instead of moments

WAKE UP TOMORROW

It is not weakness to admit this, it is awareness. Awareness is the beginning of healing. You do not have to stay in survival forever. You are not meant to only exist. You deserve a life that feeds your soul, not drains it.

Somewhere inside you is a version of you who wants more:
More peace.
More laughter.
More presence.
More love.
More rest.
More self-compassion.
More reasons to wake up joyful, not just alive.
That version of you is not gone, only buried.
She is waiting.
He is waiting.
They are waiting for space.
For healing.
For air.
For hope.
For a crack in the armor where light can enter. Survival kept you alive, honor that. But living will set you free, pursue that.

This book is your guide back to life. Back to feeling. Back to joy. Back to connection. Back to yourself. Not the you who learned to endure, but the you who deserves to live.

Slowly.
Gently.
Bravely. You survived the dark

PART XI

The Moment You Think,
"I Can't Do This Anymore"

There is a breaking point that many silent sufferers know too well, a moment where pain, exhaustion, and hopelessness intersect. It doesn't always look dramatic.

Sometimes it's quiet. Sometimes it's the moment you sit on the edge of your bed staring at the floor. Sometimes it's a shower where you let the water hide your tears. Sometimes it's lying under blankets wishing you were someone else.

This moment is not loud, it's heavy.

It sounds like:
"I can't keep living like this."
"I don't know how to survive the next hour."
"This pain is too much."
"I don't want to fight anymore."

It is not that you want life to end, you want suffering to end. You don't want to disappear, you want the weight to stop crushing you. You want relief. Rest. Release from the constant internal battle.

People often think suicidal thoughts are chosen, but they are not born from desire. They are born from ***overwhelm.***

WAKE UP TOMORROW

The human heart can only hold so much before it cracks. The mind can only fight so long before it collapses. The soul can only endure so many storms before it needs shelter.

When you reach the point of "I can't do this anymore," it is not weakness, it is a sign your pain has run beyond capacity. No one collapses because they are weak, they collapse because they've been strong for too long.

You've held it together. You've fought battle after battle alone. You've survived trauma others didn't see. You've carried weights people assumed you could handle. And when you finally break, you blame yourself for shattering. But breaking is human. Crying is release, and feeling defeated is a signal, not a flaw.

It means your heart is asking for help.
It means you can't keep walking alone.
It means healing needs to begin beyond your own strength.

Pain says: "End it."

But truth whispers: "End the pain — not your life."

There is a difference.
A vital one.
A lifesaving one.

You don't need to die, you need support.
You need rest.
You need space to fall apart safely.
You need connection.
You need someone to sit with you in the dark until your strength returns.

The moment you think "I can't do this anymore" is often the moment right before something shifts. Right before a breakthrough. Right before help arrives. Right before the storm begins to calm. Right before you choose to stay just one more day.

One more day can change everything.
One more day could introduce you to someone who saves your life.
One more day could bring a memory worth living for.
One more day could lead you into treatment, therapy, healing.
One more day could be the day the weight gets lighter.

You don't have to do this anymore **alone**.
But you do have to stay.

You don't need strength for a year, just for one more moment. Just enough to breathe. Just enough to not act on the thought.

You're allowed to say: "I need help." "I'm not okay." "This is too heavy for me."

Those words do not mean you surrender; they are survival.

One day you will look back and be grateful you didn't give up here. Grateful you stayed long enough to see life soften. Grateful you lived long enough to feel joy again.

Because pain ends.
Seasons change.
Storms pass.
Hearts rebuild.

Your story is not done.
Not today.
Not here.

"I can't do this anymore" doesn't mean you should leave —
it means you've reached the moment to reach out.

This chapter is your reminder:

There is another way out that doesn't require dying.
There is help.
There is hope.
There is healing.

Stay.

"The pain you feel today is the strength you'll feel tomorrow."

- Author Unknown

Chapter 4:

When The Mind Won't Stop
(The Spiral Of Overthinking)

<u>PART I</u>

When someone is hurting silently, the battlefield is not outside, it's inside the mind. Thoughts don't come one at a time. They come in waves. Rushing. Recycling. Repeating.

Overthinking turns minutes into hours.
Nights into storms.
Silence into screaming.

You lie awake while the world sleeps, heart racing, mind spinning, like a room with no doors, only corners.

Every thought echoes: "Why am I like this?" "What's wrong with me?" "Why can't I get it together?" "What if I always feel this way?"

Pain becomes a loop; not loud, but constant. Not violent but draining. Not dramatic, but heavy. Overthinking attacks from two angles:

The past: replaying moments you can't change, mistakes you regret, memories that haunt, and words that cut deep.

The future: imagining pain ahead, failure waiting, abandonment looming, uncertainty suffocating.

The mind travels everywhere except where the body is, here.

Now.

Overthinking convinces you that: Pain is permanent. Nothing will change. You're stuck where you are. You'll always feel this way.

But feelings are not facts, even when they feel overwhelming.

The spiral begins subtly:

A thought.
A worry.
A what-if.
A memory.
A fear.

Then suddenly you're drowning in it, without ever moving from your bed. Overthinking is not weakness; it is a tired mind trying to solve pain alone. A mind trying to make sense of chaos. Trying to protect itself. Trying to predict hurt before it happens again. But protection becomes prison.

Your brain begins preparing for the future by reliving the past, repeatedly, believing if it can understand the pain, it can prevent more pain. But instead, it multiplies pain.

This spiral is why suicidal thoughts feel like an exit. Not because life is unwanted, but because the mental noise is unbearable. The exhaustion isn't physical, it's emotional.

Soul deep.
Bone heavy.
Spirit tired.

The mind says: "I can't carry these thoughts anymore." "I just want quiet." "I just want peace." And that quiet is imagined in the wrong direction, toward disappearance instead of healing. But there *is* another way.

The mind can rest.
Thoughts can soften.
Spirals can slow. Peace can be found in life, not loss.

It begins with awareness: "I'm spiraling." "I need to pause." "This thought is heavy, but it is not truth." And slowly, gently, compassionately, you learn to interrupt the spiral. Not by force, but by understanding. The goal is not to silence the mind immediately, but to offer it a different voice: "You are safe." "You are here." "This moment is temporary." "Pain is passing through, not permanent."

Your brain is noisy because it's afraid.
Because it cares.
Because it wants relief.

You are not broken, you are overwhelmed. And that is treatable.
Interruptible.
Shiftable.
Healable.

Your thoughts are loud today, but they do not define your tomorrow.

<u>PART II</u>

When Thoughts Become Too Loud To Carry Alone

There is a point where pain stops whispering and begins to roar. Where thoughts no longer sit quietly in the mind but pound inside the skull like fists against a locked door. Where emotions no longer ache, they scream. You try to distract yourself.

You....
Scroll.
Sleep.
Clean.
Work.
Stay busy.

But distraction only quiets the noise temporarily, like muting a television instead of turning it off. The moment silence returns; the thoughts return with it: "What's wrong with me?" "Why can't I get better?" "Maybe everyone is better without me." "Maybe peace is somewhere I can't reach."

It's not that you want to die, you just can't imagine living like this indefinitely. When thoughts become too loud, they stop sounding like thoughts and start sounding like truth. The mind becomes both the injury and the wound. The critic and the judge. The attacker and the victim.

You battle yourself all day, then collapse at night too tired to dream. You survive another morning, but your soul hasn't tasted rest in a long time. There is only so much a human heart can hold alone. Pain expands in isolation. Thoughts multiply in darkness. Silence feeds the suffering. Carrying everything alone turns emotional weight into suffocation.

This is where suicidal thoughts often grow roots, not out of desire, but out of overwhelm.

The brain says: "I can't carry this anymore." "I need relief now." "I'm so tired of hurting." And without support, relief looks like escape. Not because escape is what you want, but because support feels unavailable. Because asking for help feels terrifying. Because silence feels safer, even when it hurts.

But hear this truth clearly: When the thoughts are too loud to carry alone, that is *not failure.* That is a signal. A signal that you need support. A signal that the load is heavier than one heart should carry. A signal that help is not only allowed, but also necessary. Humans were not designed to heal in isolation. We were built for connection.

For community.
For shared burdens.

Sometimes healing starts with admitting: "This is too heavy for me alone." Not as weakness, but as wisdom. When thoughts are loud, another voice can soften the noise. A therapist can help you untangle the knots. A friend can remind you that you matter. A support group can help you feel less alone. A prayer can restore hope when you feel empty.

WAKE UP TOMORROW

Help is not a sign you are broken; help is a bridge toward safety, stability, and peace.

Even warriors need medics.
Even strong trees need water.
Even survivors deserve rest.

If your thoughts feel too loud right now, this page is your hand to hold. You do not have to carry this by yourself anymore. There is support. There is help. There is healing. There is tomorrow.

Your life is bigger than the thoughts attacking you. The storm in your mind is not the end of your story. Let someone stand with you in the rain. You were never meant to weather every storm alone.

PART III

The Night Thoughts Hit Hardest
(Why Evenings Are Emotionally Dangerous)

Pain feels different at night.

During the day, life is noisy, calls coming in, kids needing things, work demanding you, scrolling feeds, errands to run, tasks to complete.

Daytime offers distraction.
Noise.
Movement.
Purpose, even forced purpose.

But night removes all of that. The world grows quiet, phones stop buzzing, people go home, and the mind is left alone with itself. That's when thoughts get loud and the questions you avoided all day find you.

The memories you buried rise to the surface. The insecurities whisper. The trauma knocks. The loneliness enters the room like a shadow. Nothing competes with the noise in your head anymore.

The dark makes everything feel heavier, every mistake bigger, every heartbreak deeper, and every worry more real. You stare at the ceiling, counting regrets instead of sheep. You scroll until your eyes burn, hoping numbness arrives before sleep. You replay conversations, imagine futures that scare you, and feel emotions you spent the day running from. Night has a way of making pain feel infinite. Suddenly you're not just tired, you're empty. Not just sad, you're sinking. Not just overwhelmed, you're drowning.

The silence becomes suffocating, and the mind becomes its own echo chamber. This is why so many suicidal thoughts surface at night. Not because pain increases, but because distractions decrease. The brain begins to wander into "what if" territory:

"What if I disappeared?"
"What if I just stopped fighting?"
"What if peace is never going to come while I'm alive?"
Not out of desire to die, but out of exhaustion from surviving.

Nighttime becomes negotiation: "One more day... or is this the last?" "I'll just sleep and maybe I won't wake up." "I can't keep doing this." These thoughts are not weakness, they are signals. Signals that the heart is tired and needs help. Signals that healing is urgent, not optional.

If this is familiar, hear me:
The night is a moment, not the truth.
Darkness changes perception.
Loneliness distorts reality.
Pain magnifies in silence.
But morning always comes.

Thoughts that feel permanent at 2 a.m. look different at 10 a.m. after breakfast, sunlight, conversation, and breath. Night is when you need comfort the most, not solutions, not lectures, just comfort.

A blanket around your body.
A warm drink.
A journal.
A prayer.
A song that calms your spirit.
A voice reminding you you're not alone.

Night does not have to win.
Darkness is not the end.
Thoughts are not commands; they are symptoms.

Symptoms of pain.
Symptoms of exhaustion.

Not identity.
Not destiny.

And if you are reading this late at night, with swollen eyes or a heavy chest, wondering how long you can keep going, stay for the morning. Stay for one more sunrise. Stay for one more laugh. Stay for the future that pain can't see yet.

Stay because the story isn't finished.
Stay because hope might return tomorrow.
Stay because healing happens slowly, but surely.

You deserve to see what peace looks like in daylight.

<u>PART IV</u>

When Sleep Feels Like Escape
(The Desire to Disappear Into Rest)

There's a difference between being tired and being tired of being alive. One is physical. The other is soul deep.

When someone is emotionally exhausted, sleep becomes more than rest. It becomes a *refuge*. A hiding place. A temporary escape from the world that keeps demanding more than they must give.

Sleeping late.
Napping often.
Staying in bed all day.
Not wanting to get up.
Going back to sleep to avoid the day.

It might look like laziness from the outside, but internally, it's survival. Rest is the only place where pain pauses, where thoughts soften, where the world disappears long enough for the heart to breathe. For a moment, there is peace.

No arguments.
No expectations.
No memories replaying.
No pressure to smile or function.

Just nothingness.
Just quiet.

So, sleep becomes escape. Not because someone wants to live in dreams, but because waking feels like returning to war.

You wake up and the weight returns instantly:
The thoughts.
The shame.
The overwhelm.
The responsibilities.

The bills.
The trauma.
The loneliness.
The memories.

You'll have to wear the mask again.

So, you roll over, pull the blanket up, and hope sleep takes you back under, where the world can't reach you. Sometimes the most dangerous thought is not death, but "I wish I could sleep forever."

It sounds gentle, harmless even. But beneath it lives a deeper hope:

"I wish I could stop hurting."
"I wish I could disappear without dying."
"I wish I didn't have to face tomorrow."

This is not a desire for an ending; it is a desire for *pause.*

A break from being strong.
A break from feeling everything.
A break from pretending you're okay.
A break from being responsible for your survival.

If anyone has ever felt this, know:

WAKE UP TOMORROW

You are not lazy.
You are not weak.
You are not failing at life.
You are tired, deeply, emotionally tired.
Your mind is asking for relief.
Your body is begging for peace.
Your soul is exhausted from holding pain with no place to set it down.

And that exhaustion deserves compassion, not shame. But while sleep can soothe, it cannot heal.

You cannot rest away trauma.
You cannot sleep away grief.
You cannot nap through depression.
You cannot dream your way out of pain.

Rest can support you, but recovery requires more than hiding. Healing begins when we learn to find peace *awake*, not only asleep. When you slowly rebuild life into something worth waking up for. When mornings feel less like punishment and more like possibility. When getting out of bed is not a battle but a beginning.

That is where you're headed. Not overnight, not all at once but step by step, breath by breath.

For now, hear this softly:
You deserve rest, but you also deserve life.
You deserve sleep, but you also deserve mornings that don't hurt.
You deserve dreams, but you also deserve days that feel like them.
Sleep may be escape temporarily, but healing will be your escape permanently.

One day you'll rise not because you must, but because you want to. One day you'll wake up excited for tomorrow, not trying to avoid it. One day rest will be restoration, not escape.

Hold on for that day.

PART V

When You Feel Like A Burden

One of the deepest wounds in a hurting mind is not pain, it's the belief that *you are the problem.*

Not that life is heavy, but that you are heavy.
Not that situations hurt, but that you hurt people.
Not that you are struggling, but that your struggle inconveniences others. This belief grows quietly, like mold in the corners of the heart.

It starts as a thought:
"They don't need my problems."
"They're better off without me."
Then it becomes a feeling:
"I take up too much space."
"I require too much care."
Then it becomes identity:
"I am a burden."

And when someone begins to believe they are a burden, asking for help feels like proof of the very thing they're afraid of.

Instead of reaching out, they withdraw.
Instead of crying out, they hold it in.
Instead of saying "I'm struggling," they say "I'm fine" with a smile that doesn't reach their eyes.

The mind twists the narrative:
"They love me, but I'm exhausting them."
"They support me, but I'm draining them."
"They care, but not enough to stay if they knew everything."

So instead of letting others show love, you protect them from your pain, at the cost of carrying it alone.

But here's the truth pain hides:

You are not a burden.
You are a human being in pain.

Needing support does not make you heavy, it makes you deserving of care. You are not a weight people must carry, you are a soul worthy of community, compassion, and connection.

The world taught you to believe pain should be hidden. Life tells you vulnerability is weakness. Experience makes you think your needs are too much.

But you are not "too much."
You are **important.**
Valuable.
Worth loving.
Worth helping.

And the people who are meant for you, the safe ones, the real ones will never see your struggle as inconvenience.

They will see it as invitation: to love you deeper, support you stronger, stand with you longer.

People who truly care don't feel burdened by your truth, they feel honored that you trust them enough to share it. You are not asking for too much.

You are asking for what every human deserves:
Love.
Support.
Understanding.
Presence.
Compassion.

If someone ever made you feel like a burden, it says more about their capacity than your worth. There are people who will hold space for you softly. People who will listen to your story without flinching. People who will sit in the dark with you until light returns.

You deserve to find them. You deserve to be that for yourself, too.
Imagine if your younger self walked up to you right now…

Small.
Sad.
Hurting.
Afraid.

Would you call them a burden?
Would you shame them for needing love?
Would you push them away and tell them to be strong alone?

No.

You would hold them. Comfort them. Protect them.

Wipe their tears. Tell them they matter. That same compassion belongs to you now.

You are not a burden; you are a soul worth saving. A story is still being written. A heart is still learning to heal. The world is better with you in it. Someone needs your laugh, your wisdom, your future, your light. Even if you can't see your worth right now, it is still there. Still shining beneath the pain.

You are not a weight. You are someone worth fighting for, including by you.

<u>PART VI</u>

When You Can't Explain Why You're Hurting

There is a unique kind of pain that confuses even the one who carries it. Not triggered by one event. Not linked to a recent loss. Not tied to a specific experience you can point to and say, "That's when it started."

Sometimes you hurt, and you don't know why. And that kind of pain can feel even heavier. Because when you can't explain it, you feel less entitled to feel it. You question yourself. You minimize your experience.

You say things like:
"I shouldn't feel this way."
"Others have it worse."
"I don't even know what's wrong with me."
"Why am I like this for no reason?"
So instead of speaking it, you suppress it.

But here's a truth the world fails to mention: You do not need a reason to hurt. Pain does not always announce itself with trauma. Depression does not always enter through a major event. Hopelessness does not always need a story to justify its presence.

Sometimes hurt comes from years of being strong. From needs that went unmet. From love that was never received properly. From boundaries you never learned to set. From childhood wounds that never healed. From exhaustion accumulated over time.

Not one big wound, a thousand tiny ones. Paper cuts of the soul.

So, when someone asks, "Why are you sad?" you genuinely don't know how to answer. Because the answer isn't linear. It isn't logical. It isn't simple.

It's layered.
Complex.
Woven through years.
Hidden beneath smiles.

Pain is not always loud, sometimes it's vague. Heaviness with no name. A sadness with no reason. A cloud with no rain, just gray. And that makes you feel alone in it.

Because how do you tell someone:
"I feel empty, but nothing happened."
"I have everything I need, but I'm still hurting."
"I should be happy, but I can't feel it."

These sentences scare people, including you. So, you say nothing. But unspoken pain grows. It sits inside the chest like a stone, pressing against your lungs, making every breath feel too small.

You begin to think: "If I can't explain it, no one will understand it." "If I can't understand it, I must be the problem." But you are not the problem. Pain without reason is still pain. Sadness without cause is still sadness. Struggle without explanation is still valid.

You don't need permission to feel.
You don't need evidence to hurt.
You don't need a story to justify your suffering.

Sometimes the body remembers what the mind has forgotten. Sometimes the heart breaks from old wounds never given time to mend. Sometimes exhaustion speaks louder than logic.

Healing begins not with explanation, but with acknowledgment. "I'm hurting, and I don't know why, but it matters." Let that sentence be enough.

You deserve compassion even when you cannot articulate what's wrong. You deserve support even if you can't name the pain. You deserve love even when you feel unlovable. You don't have to understand the hurt to heal from it.

Sometimes healing precedes understanding.
Sometimes clarity comes later.
Sometimes you grow out of pain before you ever figure out where it came from.

What matters is this:
Your pain is real. Your feelings are valid. Your struggle is seen, even when silent. You are allowed to seek help even without a reason. You are allowed to talk about your emotions even when they make no sense. You are allowed to heal even when you don't know from what. You don't need a story. You need space. You need safety. You need support.

And you deserve all three.

<u>PART VII</u>

When You Start To Believe Everyone Is Better Off Without You

This is one of the darkest thoughts people rarely admit out loud: "They would be fine without me." "Maybe I'm holding everyone back." "I cause more pain by staying than I would by leaving." It doesn't appear suddenly, it grows slowly, like vines around the mind.

It begins with exhaustion. Then shame. Then feeling misunderstood. Then believing you are too much, too emotional, too damaged.

Then the thought forms: "What if my absence is less painful than my presence?"

Not because you don't love people, but because you think you *are burdened* by your existence.

This belief is not truth. It's pain talking. Trauma talking. Exhaustion talking. But when the mind is tired, lies feel like logic.

You start looking at your relationships differently:

- When someone forgets to check on you, you take it as proof.
- When you struggle, you feel guilty for needing support.
- When people are busy, you assume you're not important.
- When someone pulls away, you blame yourself.

You begin to feel like a shadow following others, not a person they want.

WAKE UP TOMORROW

Slowly the inner dialogue shifts:
"I'm in the way."
"I'm a disappointment."
"They deserve better than me."
"Maybe my absence would bring them peace."
These thoughts are heavy.
Dangerous.
Seductive.

They offer a false promise: "If I disappear, no one gets hurt anymore." But reality speaks differently:

When someone dies by suicide, the pain doesn't leave, it transfers. To the mother who will replay every memory, wondering what she missed. To the child who grows up believing they weren't worth staying for. To the friend who thinks, "I should have called." To the spouse who carries the weight of unanswered questions forever.

Suicide doesn't remove pain; it explodes it into everyone who loves you. You are not removing yourself from the burden, you are becoming their burden of grief, guilt, and trauma for the rest of their lives.

Not intentionally.
Not selfishly.
But painfully, tragically.

Because you didn't want to die.
You wanted peace.
And no one taught you how to find it alive.

The truth is:

People are not better without you. They break without you. They search for you in empty chairs, in old voicemails, in holidays with a missing seat, in dreams where you still exist. Your presence may feel heavy, but your absence would be unbearable.

You matter more than you think.
You contribute more than you know.
You hold space in people's hearts you don't realize you occupy.

Your story is not over.
Your life is not disposable.
Your worth is not measured by how much you struggle.

You being here is not a burden, it's a blessing someone hasn't said aloud in the way you need to hear.

If no one has told you recently:
You make the world warmer by existing.
You bring a light you cannot see in yourself right now.
Your future self is cheering for you, begging you to stay.
Someone's healing will come from your testimony.
Someone's life will be saved because you survived.
You think you take up too much space, but someone is praying for you to stay in it.

Life is not better without you. Someone out there needs you to live long enough to love them or be loved by them. Someone hasn't met you yet and will thank God for your existence. Someone will breathe easier because you chose tomorrow.

Hold on.

WAKE UP TOMORROW

Not for perfection, for possibility.
For the versions of you that haven't been born yet.
For the joys you haven't felt yet.
For mornings that don't hurt.
For a peace that doesn't require disappearing.

You are not better gone.
You are needed here.

PART VIII

The Turning Point
A Spark, A Voice, A Pause

Every breaking point carries a hidden crossroads. It doesn't come with bright lights, dramatic music, or a loud voice from heaven. Sometimes it appears small, so small you could miss it if you blink.

A spark instead of a flame.
A whisper instead of a shout.
A tiny thread of hope instead of a rope to climb.

The turning point isn't always a rescue. Sometimes it's a pause. A moment where something, anything, interrupts the spiral long enough to hold on. It might be a text from someone at the right time. A memory of laughter. A picture of your child. A scripture you remember. A friend calling your name. A voice inside saying, "Not yet." A thought as light as a feather saying, "Maybe tomorrow."

Not a full reason to live, just a reason to wait. And waiting saves lives.

Staying for one more hour.
One more sunrise.
One more conversation.
One more chance at peace.

Sometimes the turning point is noticing your own tears and thinking, "I don't want to die, I want this pain to stop." Sometimes it's the moment you realize you don't want to disappear, you want someone to notice you're disappearing.

Sometimes it's simply breathing deeper than the panic, crying until exhaustion makes sleep possible, and waking with 5% more hope than yesterday. A spark doesn't heal everything, but it begins something.

Healing never enters like floodwater. It enters like a drop. Light doesn't remove darkness instantly, it pierces it. Hope doesn't always roar, sometimes it flickers.

A pause is powerful.

The spiral breaks.
The mind catches breath.
A moment of clarity breaks through the noise.

You think:
"Maybe I can try again tomorrow."
"Maybe there's still something left for me."
"Maybe someone would miss me."
"Maybe this isn't the end."

The turning point is not being healed, it is being willing to imagine healing is possible. Not certainty, possibility. A small thought like, "What if I stay?" And staying opens the door for support.

For therapy.
For faith.
For community.
For medication.

For coping skills.
For connection.

A tiny spark can become a flame.

You do not need to feel strong to reach a turning point.
You only need to feel willing, even slightly, to pause.

Sometimes survival comes down to the smallest truth:
You matter.
Your life is important.
Pain is not permanent.
Darkness is not final.
This moment is not your whole story.
The turning point is the moment you choose possibility over ending.
Not forever, just now.

Hope grows from moments like this, quiet, unexpected, fragile, real. And one day, you will look back on this moment, the moment you paused instead of ending, the moment you stayed one more night, and see it for what it truly was: the start of your return to life. Your spark. Your shift. Your turning point.

The beginning of healing.

<u>*Closing Summary:*</u>

The Mind, The Battle, The Turning Point

In this chapter, we walked through one of the hardest places a human heart can go: inside the mind of suicidal pain. We explored the quiet war that often lives behind a functional face. The exhaustion hidden behind smiles.

WAKE UP TOMORROW

The nights when thoughts are loud and rooms feel too dark. The moments where living feels heavy and sleep feels like escape. The belief that others would be better without you, a lie pain tells in your most fragile hour.

We acknowledged that suicidal thoughts are not about wanting death but wanting *relief.* Not about disappearing but wanting the pain to stop.

We saw how overthinking spirals, how burdens feel unbearable, how hopelessness blinds the future, how "I can't do this anymore" becomes a whisper of surrender.

But this chapter did not end there. It led us to the turning point, that tiny spark that interrupts the spiral.

A pause.
A reason to wait one more night.
A whisper of hope instead of a scream of despair.

Because healing rarely enters loudly, it begins with a moment.

A deep breath.
A text.
A tear.
A memory.
A prayer.
A pause.

A small decision that says, "Not today. Maybe tomorrow. Let me stay one more moment." And that moment becomes life.

This chapter was not written to romanticize pain, but to validate its reality, to name it, to bring it into light, to remove shame from struggle, and remind you that being overwhelmed is human.

What you felt does not make you weak. The thoughts you've had do not make you broken. The nights you survived alone do not make you unworthy. You are still here. And that matters.

Now we move into what comes next, the rebuilding. Because understanding the darkness is only the first half of the journey. The next is learning how to step toward the light. You've walked through the mental landscape of suicidal thought, now Chapter Five will begin by teaching you how to climb out of it.

How to cope.
How to ask for help.
How to speak your pain aloud.
How to restore hope.
How to create safety.
How to rebuild yourself gently, piece by piece.
How to live again, not just survive.

You made it through this chapter. That alone is victory.

Take a deep breath.
You don't have to rush.
You don't have to be okay yet.

You must stay.

Tomorrow is waiting for you, and Chapter Five will help you meet it.

Chapter 5:

Coming Back to Yourself:
Learning To Reach For Help, Hold On, & Heal

<u>PART I</u>

Healing begins quietly.

Not with fireworks or drastic change, but with the smallest shift, a breath you didn't think you had left, a morning you didn't plan to wake for, a thought that whispers, "Maybe I could try again."

After surviving long nights, deep spirals, and thoughts that nearly ended it all, you don't need perfection, you need permission.

Permission to heal slowly.
Permission to ask for help.
Permission to not have all the answers.
Permission to rest.
Permission to begin again, even if today feels fragile.

Some people were never taught how to lean on others. They learned strength as survival, resilience as requirement, and independence as armor. If that's you, this chapter is not asking you to put your strength down, only to stop carrying everything alone.

You don't have to be the strong one here.
You don't have to have it together.
You don't have to know what you need, you must be willing to let someone in, even slightly.

Healing will require both:
The **soft work** within yourself
and
The **brave work** of reaching outward.

Because recovery is not built in isolation, it is built in connection, care, and courage. You may not feel ready for big steps yet, and that's okay. This chapter is about *small* steps that save lives.

Healing looks like:
- Drinking water even when you don't feel thirsty
- Opening curtains to let sunlight into the room
- Answering one message instead of all of them
- Taking a shower after three heavy days
- Lying in bed and breathing deeply for five minutes
- Asking someone, "Can you sit with me while I feel this?"
- Saying the hardest words: "I need help."

Tiny victories count as evidence of life returning. And when your mind spirals again, because healing is not linear, you'll also have *tools*, not just hope.

Tools for grounding when thoughts are loud:
- Press your feet flat to the floor
- Name five things you see
- Place your hand over your heart
- Breathe in for 4, hold for 4, release for 6
- Repeat: "This moment is temporary."

Tools for reaching out when isolation tempts you:
- Text a friend: "Can you check on me? I'm struggling today."
- Call someone you trust, even if you have no words
- Tell a therapist, pastor, or support group what you're carrying
- Say "I need help" instead of "I'm fine" even once

Tools for survival when holding on hurts:

- Delay any harmful urge by ten minutes
- Place cold water on your wrists or face to disrupt panic
- Write your feelings instead of acting on them
- Create a crisis safety plan (we'll build one together later)
- Sit in the discomfort, it will pass, even if slowly

You deserve coping tools in your hand, not pain alone in your chest.

This chapter will guide you towards:
- How to ask for help without guilt
- How to identify safe people
- How to create a crisis plan for dangerous nights
- How to rebuild your identity after survival mode
- How to reconnect with joy, purpose, and self-love
- How to remember you are worth staying for

You are not weak for needing support, you are wise to recognize where healing begins. You are not behind, you're alive. That is progress.

You are not starting from zero, you're rising from a place many people never survive. This chapter is your return to your body, your heart, your voice, your life.

Slowly.
Gently.
Bravely.

The journey ahead won't be perfect, but it will be real, transformative, and yours. You survived the darkness. Now we walk toward the light, one small step at a time.

PART II

How To Ask For Help When You Don't Know What To Say

Asking for help is one of the hardest things to do when you're hurting. Not because you don't need support but because you don't know how to express what feels indescribable.

How do you explain heaviness without a reason? How do you say you're drowning when you look like you're standing fine? How do you ask for comfort without feeling like a burden?

You may sit with the phone in your hand, typing a message and deleting it. You may rehearse a call in your mind but never press "dial." You may wish someone would just notice without you having to speak. But healing requires connection, and connection requires opening the door, even slightly. This chapter teaches practical ways to reach out, even when speaking feels impossible.

1. You Don't Need Perfect Words, Just Honest Ones

You don't have to tell your life story.
You don't need a speech.
You don't even need clarity, just willingness.

Help can sound like:
"I'm not okay. Can you talk to me for a bit?"
"I don't know how to explain it, but I'm struggling."

"I need company. Can you sit with me, even quietly?"
"Can you check on me later today?"
"Can I come over? I don't want to be alone."
Short. True. Human.

2. Safe People Aren't Perfect — They're Present

Look for people who:
- Listen instead of fix
- Validate instead of judge
- Stay instead of shrink
- Handle your truth gently

Not everyone is safe, and that's okay. We're seeking **one or two people,** not the world.

Write this list in your notes or journal:
Who makes me feel seen?
Who makes me feel safe?
Who can I be honest with?
Their names matter, they are lifelines, not crowds.

3. You Can Ask for the Type of Support You Need

Support isn't one size fits all.
Some moments require listening.
Some require distraction.
Some require presence.

Try phrases like:

For listening:
"I just need someone to hear me, not solve me."

For comfort:
"Can you sit with me through this?"

For motivation:
"Can you remind me why my life matters today?"

For distraction:
"Can you help me get through the next hour?"

Let people love you in the way you need.

4. If Speaking is Too Hard, Use Alternatives

Healing doesn't always start with conversation.

You can ask for support through:

- A text
- A voice memo
- A note
- A letter
- A forwarded quote that says what you feel
- A simple emoji that means "check on me"

Sometimes help begins with one notification. You are not required to bleed publicly, you are only asked not to bleed *alone*.

5. You Are Not a Burden, You're a Human Being

Asking for help is not weakness, it's courage wearing vulnerability.

You deserve support.
You deserve presence.
You deserve love in real time, not after a tragedy.

You are worth reaching for, even when it feels uncomfortable.

This chapter is your permission:
To text.
To call.
To say, "I need you."
Not because you can't stand alone, but because you don't have to.

PART III

Rebuilding Yourself After Survival Mode

Survival mode teaches you how to endure, how to wake up hurting and function anyway, how to swallow emotions and keep going, how to smile without feeling joy, how to live without really living. It keeps you alive, but it also disconnects you from yourself.

When pain becomes constant, you stop noticing who you are beneath it. Your personality dulls. Your needs disappear behind responsibility. Your dreams shrink to fit inside survival.

But healing is not just about staying alive. it's about coming back to life.

This part of your journey is about **rebuilding**, not into your old self, but into the version of you who grows from everything you survived. Not who you were before the pain, but who you are becoming because of it.

<u>**Step 1**</u>: Meet Yourself Where You Are — Not Where You "Should Be"

<u>**Step 2**</u>: Reconnect With Your Body

<u>**Step 3**</u>: Rediscover What Brings You Peace

<u>**Step 4**</u>: Create Small Routines That Ground You

Step 5: Speak out loud: "This feeling is temporary. I only need to survive this moment."

Step 6: Contact someone from a list of trusted people.

You are allowed to interrupt your thoughts; a pause can save a life.

<u>PART IV</u>

Learning To Trust Yourself With Life Again

Healing doesn't just require staying alive, it requires believing you can live.

Not perfectly.
Not fearlessly.
Not instantly.

Just believing it's possible, even if your voice shakes while saying it. When you've spent months, years, even decades in emotional survival, trusting yourself can feel dangerous.

What if I break again?
What if I fall back into the darkness?
What if the thoughts return?
What if I can't handle life when it gets heavy?

These questions are normal.
Real.
Human.

You're learning to hold your life with open hands again, not gripping it in panic, not dropping it in despair, but carrying it gently, like something fragile turning strong.

You are not trying to become "the old you."
You are building a *new* you, brick by brick, breath by breath.

A version that knows:
I can feel deeply without drowning.
I can ask for help without shame.
I can fall apart and recover.
I can face hard moments and still choose tomorrow.
I can trust myself with the life I fought to keep.
Trust is not built by believing you'll never break again, but by knowing you can survive it if you do.

Truth says:
"I am learning to trust myself." Make it gentle.
Make it reassuring.
Make it yours.

PART IV

Relearning Joy: Learning To Live Again After Wanting To Die

There comes a moment in healing where the question shifts from:

"How do I survive?"
to
"How do I live?"

For so long, life felt like something you had to endure; a test of strength, not an experience of fullness. You survived on autopilot. You kept breathing, but you weren't alive inside. Now comes the fragile, sacred work of rebuilding life with intention. And that begins with *joy.*

Not forced joy.
Not fake smiles.
Not pretending everything is okay.

But soft joy.
Slow joy.
Real joy, the kind that sneaks back like sunrise after a long night.

Joy After Darkness Feels Strange At First

When you have lived close to death, pleasure can feel undeserved. You might catch yourself laughing and immediately feel guilty. You might enjoy something small and then wonder, "Am I allowed to feel happy after everything?" You may fear that joy won't last, so you hold it at arm's length, just in case.

This is normal.

Healing may bring moments of light, but the body isn't used to it yet. Joy can feel unfamiliar, like stepping into warm water after years of cold. Allow yourself to adjust, receive softness slowly and believe that happiness isn't a trap, it's your right.

Chapter 6:

Who Am I Now?
Reclaiming Identity After Survival

<u>PART I</u>

When you've lived in darkness for a long time, healing can feel like stepping into a world you don't recognize. And when you survive what once tried to end you, you don't walk out the same person who walked in.

You change.
Your heart changes.
Your priorities shift.
Your soul rearranges itself.

Pain transforms you, not just in the breaking, but in the rebuilding. This chapter is where we explore who you are now, not who you were before the trauma, not who pain convinced you to become, but who you are as a survivor, a healer, a rising soul.

You are no longer the version of you who wished for the end. You are the version who chose to stay. There is power in that.

You Don't Have To Go Back You Get To Go Forward

People often say, "I just want to feel like myself again."

But the truth is: You are not meant to return to the person you were before the heartbreak, before the depression, before the crisis. That version of you didn't know what you know now. Didn't carry this strength. Didn't hold this depth. Didn't understand the value of breath and tomorrow.

You're not going back, you're becoming. Not a restoration of who you were, but an evolution into someone new.

Someone softer.

Someone wiser.

Someone stronger.

Someone who tastes life differently now.

Write new language for yourself:

"I am a survivor, not a statistic."

"I am healing, not hopeless."

"I am growing, not stuck."

"I am worthy, not burdensome."

Identity begins in words. Pain used to drown your voice out. Now we learn to listen to it again.

Releasing The Versions Of You That Had To Survive

There is a version of you who held everything together. Who didn't ask for help. Who swallowed pain to protect others. Who smiled while breaking quietly.

Honor them, they kept you alive. But you don't have to be her forever. You can lay down her armor. You can loosen her grip. You can thank her for surviving and let yourself grow beyond survival. Step into the version of you who gets to live, not just endure.

Identity Through Joy, Not Just Trauma

Instead of defining yourself by what hurts you, define yourself by what lights you up.

Ask:

- What makes me feel alive?
- What makes me feel alive?

- What makes me feel safe?
- What could I do for hours and lose track of time?
- What hobbies have I abandoned that deserve revival?

Maybe you're creative.

Maybe you're nurturing.

Maybe you're a writer.

A leader.

A healer.

A thinker.

A feeler. Maybe you don't know yet, and that's beautiful. Discovery happens in living.

Stand Tall in Who You Are Becoming

Identity after survival is not about perfection, it's about authenticity. About learning to show up as yourself, without shrinking, apologizing, or performing.

You get to:

- Say no
- Set boundaries
- Take up space
- Protect your peace
- Trust your voice
- Live without guilt
- Choose joy
- Become new

Your story doesn't end at survival, it begins there. You are not broken, you are unfolding.

PART II

Becoming Someone You Love Worthiness, Boundaries, And Building Life Day By Day

Healing is not just about staying alive —
it's about learning to live in a way that feels worth waking up for.

Not a perfect life.
Not a pain-free life.
But a life that feels like **yours**.

This part of your journey asks a new question:

"How do I become someone I am proud to be — someone I love?"

You have spent years surviving.
Now you are learning how to value yourself, honor yourself, and build a life that reflects your worth.

This is not selfish —
this is sacred.

Self-Worth After Survival

When you've wanted to die, self-worth can feel distant.

You may look in the mirror and see someone tired, broken, or unlovable —
because you saw yourself through the lens of pain for so long.

But hear this clearly:

You are not unworthy —
you are unhealed.

Your value was never erased by your struggle.

You mattered on your darkest day
just as much as you matter now.

Self-worth grows slowly —
through acts of care, not perfection.

It sounds like:

"I deserve kindness — even from myself."
"My needs matter."
"I am worthy of help, rest, love, and joy."

You don't become worthy —
you **realize you already are.**

Loving Yourself Is a Relationship

Just like loving another person takes time,
loving yourself does too.

It means:

- Showing up for yourself daily
- Apologizing to yourself for past neglect
- Caring for your body, mind, and soul
- Being patient when progress is slow
- Speaking gently to the voice inside

It means treating yourself like someone you are learning to love —
not someone you are trying to fix.

Ask:

"How can I be kinder to myself today?"

Some days love looks like bubble baths and candles, other days it looks like drinking water and opening the curtains. Both count.

Boundaries: A Form of Self-Love, Not Selfishness

Setting boundaries means: "I honor myself enough to protect my peace." You are not responsible for making everyone comfortable. You are responsible for keeping yourself alive, whole, and safe.

Boundaries sound like:
"No, I can't do that today."
"I need time to rest."
"I'm not available for conversations that harm me."
"I love you, but I cannot self-abandon for you."
The old you survived by pleasing people.
The healed you learns to choose yourself.
Not to push others away —
but to stop pushing **yourself** aside.

Rebuilding Life Day By Day

Life after wanting to die is not about giant transformation, it's about consistent small choices that teach your brain: "I'm staying."

Building life looks like:
- Cooking your own meals
- Making goals for the week
- Journaling before panic escalates
- Scheduling therapy or support groups

- Creating routines that bring balance
- Saying yes to things that grow you
- Saying no to what drains you
- Trying new experiences without needing perfection

Healing is everyday effort, not one big moment. Some days you'll take steps forward. Some days you'll rest. Some days you'll break down and rebuild again. None of these are failures, they are *human.*

Becoming Someone You're Proud Of

Loving yourself isn't about appearance, success, or productivity. It's about alignment.

Ask yourself:
"What kind of person do I want to be now?"
"How do I want to show up in the world?"
"What would a healed version of me do today?"

You are rewriting your story, not erasing the past, but transforming it. Your scars are not shame; they are evidence that you survived. You are allowed to be proud of that. One day, you will look in the mirror and see:

- ✓ Strength
- ✓ Softness
- ✓ Worth
- ✓ Life
- ✓ Courage
- ✓ Growth

And you'll realize that you didn't just survive, You *became.*

WAKE UP TOMORROW

I am learning To Love You Because...

Examples:
- because you stayed
- because you're trying
- because you're healing
- because you deserve softness

Affirmation:
I am becoming someone I am proud to love. My worth is non-negotiable. My boundaries are sacred. My life is being rebuilt with purpose, peace, and compassion.

PART III

Loving Yourself While Healing, Finding Your People,
& Designing A Life Worth Staying For

You don't wait to love yourself *after* you heal, you learn to love yourself **as you heal.** You don't wait to feel whole before showing up in relationships, you show up as you are, growing in real time. You don't wait for the perfect moment to begin living, you build life from the small, imperfect moments you have now.

Healing is not a destination; it's how you walk through your life. And now that you're learning who you are becoming, you get to create the kind of world that nourishes you.

A world where you are respected.
A world where you are safe.
A world where you are loved, including by yourself.

This chapter is about building that world.

Loving Yourself Right Here, Right Now

People often say: "I'll love myself when I'm better." "When I stop breaking down." "When I finally heal." But self-love is not the reward for healing, it's part of the healing. You don't wait until the wound is closed to care for it. You tend to it during the bleeding.

Self-love during healing looks like:

- Speaking gently to yourself when you struggle
- Forgiving yourself for slow days
- Holding space for your feelings without shame

- Treating your body with care even when you're tired
- Celebrating progress you once ignored

You are allowed to love the version of you that is still learning, still hurting, still becoming. Love is not for the final version; it is for every version. Especially this one.

You Deserve Relationships That Feel Like Home

After surviving pain, you see people differently.

You no longer have energy for half-love.
For conditional support.
For relationships where you bleed while others drink.

Healing teaches you to choose:

- ✓ Presence over proximity
- ✓ Care over convenience
- ✓ Quality over quantity
- ✓ Real support feels like peace, not tension.

People who are safe will:
- Listen without fixing
- Hold your truth with tenderness
- Celebrate your boundaries
- Check on you without being asked
- Love you for who you are, not what you give

You do not have to beg to be understood. You do not have to carry everyone to be worthy of love. You do not have to shrink to be able to stay. The right people will meet you where you are, and grow with you where you're going.

Choosing Community When Isolation Felt Safer

Isolation protected you once. It kept you alive when connection hurt too much. But survival walls eventually become emotional prisons. Healing invites you to gently open the door.

Not all at once.
Not to everyone.
But to someone.

Connection begins with small openings:
- Replying to a message instead of ignoring
- Attending a gathering for thirty minutes
- Sitting in therapy with shaking hands
- Joining one group, support, church, creative, recovery
- Making one friend feel safe to talk to
- Letting someone help you carry something

Little bridges matter. Humans heal in community, not alone in the dark. You deserve people who remind you why life is worth staying for.

Designing A Life Worth Staying For

You survived death, now you get to design life. Not the life others expect from you, life that feels like home in your soul.

Ask yourself:

✓ What do I want mornings to feel like?

✓ What brings peace into my space?
✓ What routines help me feel grounded?
✓ What goals ignite purpose inside me?

Begin shaping your future from the inside out.

A life worth living includes:

- Joy you don't need permission for
- Work or passions that align with purpose
- Friendships that support your growth
- Boundaries that protect your spirit
- Spaces where your nervous system relaxes
- Moments that make you grateful you stayed

Your new life will not appear overnight, it will be built, one thoughtful choice at a time.

Even tiny changes matter:

- A plant in your window
- A morning playlist
- A room decluttered
- A new book on your nightstand
- A dream board on your wall

Design life like art, piece by piece, we create meaning.

Becoming Your Future Self One Day At A Time

You don't have to see the entire future. You only need to know the next step.

Healing sounds like:

"What's one good thing I can do today?"
"What's one way I can show myself love?"
"What's one connection I can nurture?"
"What's one moment I can choose joy?"

Tiny shifts create new lives.

One day you'll realize you aren't surviving anymore, you're living. Not because pain disappeared, but because healing became stronger. You will wake up and love being here. Sleep because you want rest, not escape. Laugh without guilt. Say "no" without fear. Say "yes" because you're alive.

You will become someone you are proud to know.
Someone you enjoy spending time with.
Someone you choose, every day.

That is what this chapter is guiding you toward.

Not just life, a life you want.

PART IV

When Triggers Whisper And Setbacks Come: Staying Grounded In Your Healing

Healing does not erase pain, it teaches you how to carry it differently. Some days, you'll feel light and open. Other days, an unexpected memory, tone, smell, song, place, or silence can grab your nervous system by the throat and pull you back into rooms you worked hard to leave. This does *not* mean you are failing. This means you are healing.

Because only people who are healing notice when something hurts. Only people who are growing can feel the return of old wounds. Only people who are alive enough to try again experience setbacks.

Triggers don't mean you're broken, they mean your brain remembers. Setbacks don't erase progress, they invite a different response than before. This section teaches how to respond with compassion instead of shame, with tools instead of panic, with presence instead of retreating.

A Trigger Is Not A Command It's A Signal

A trigger is your body saying: "I've been here before. I want to protect you. I need comfort, not abandonment." Old pain resurfaces because the brain is wired for survival, not happiness.

When triggered, instead of:

"I'm back at square one."
"I thought I was over this."
"I'll never get better."

Try: "This feeling is familiar, not fatal." "I'm reacting to memory, not reality." "My healing hasn't disappeared; it's being tested." Reframe power.

When A Setback Hits, Never Start With Judgment

The mind will try to shame you:
"Why are you feeling like this again?"
"You should be stronger by now."
"You're slipping backward."
But shame is gasoline to the fire.

Respond to yourself like a child in pain:
"You're overwhelmed, let's slow down."
"You're safe, even if you don't feel like it."
"We've survived this feeling before."
"Let's take this minute by minute."
Speak kindly.
You need compassion, not criticism.

Allow the Emotion to Pass Through the Body

Triggers often come with:
Tight chest
Shaky hands
Stomachache
Tears
Numbness

Anger
Shutting down
Feel it without fast escape.

Sit with the emotion like a wave:
- Acknowledge it
- Breathe through it
- Let it rise and fall

Emotion held becomes trauma, but emotions processed become release.

Setbacks Are Part Of Growth, Not Proof You Haven't Healed

Imagine healing like a staircase: You climb upward, step, step, step, then suddenly you trip back two steps. It feels like failure. But you're *still higher than when you started.* One step back does not erase ten forward.

Progress looks like:
Better coping this time
Less recovery time than last year
Recognizing triggers faster
Speaking up for help
Not sinking as deep as before
You're winning quietly.

The Goal Is Not To Never Break

The Goal Is to Break Better. Breaking used to mean drowning alone.

Now breaking means:

- Reaching out
- Using your safety plan
- Breathing through waves
- Speaking truth over fear
- Holding yourself with care
- Riding the moment instead of ending it

Healing is not the absence of breaking; it's the presence of restoration. Every time you come back to yourself, you strengthen the bridge.

PART V

Reclaiming Your Voice, Your Purpose, And The Future You're Becoming

At one point, your voice lived in the shadows. You swallowed pain. You stayed quiet to survive. You minimized your need to keep peace. You learned to speak softly so your hurt wouldn't echo. But silence is what suffering demands. Voice is what healing requires.

This is the chapter where you begin to speak again, not from wounds, but from wisdom. Not from fear, but from power. You survived what tried to silence you. Now you can reclaim your sound.

Your voice is not too much.
Your truth is not inconvenient.
Your feelings are not a burden.

Every time you speak honestly, you break the agreement that pain made with your past. You replace shame with story. You replace silence with self-worth. You replace invisibility with presence. Your voice is your return.

Your Story Matters: Not Just Because You Lived It, But Because You Survived It

There are people who need the truth you carry. Someone is waiting to feel less alone. Someone is drowning in thoughts you once had. Someone needs proof that tomorrow exists. Someone needs to know healing is possible.

You are becoming the evidence.

Your story can open doors in hearts, in rooms, in your own future. Whether you share publicly or privately, in writing or in whispers, to one person or one hundred, your lived experience is powerful. Pain tried to kill you, but purpose will use what pain left behind.

Finding Purpose After Darkness

Purpose rarely arrives loud; it begins as a pull.

A nudge.
A desire.
A question.
A spark.

Maybe it's service.
Maybe it's creativity.
Maybe it's motherhood, advocacy, healing, leadership.
Maybe it's simply learning to exist peacefully.

Purpose grows from survival. Meaning grows from endurance. Calling grows from places you once thought would end you. What once almost destroyed you may now become the reason someone else keeps living.

You do not have to know your full purpose today.
You only need to be open to it.

Ask yourself:

- What am I drawn to now?
- What breaks my heart in a way that makes me want to change it?
- What experience taught me something I can help others with?
- What future version of me feels like truth?

Purpose isn't found; it's uncovered. Piece by piece. Moment by moment.

Becoming Your Future Self

Close your eyes for a moment and imagine:
The healed you.
The soft you.
The strong you.
The peaceful you.
The joyful you.

The version who wakes with gratitude, speaks with clarity, loves without abandoning herself. She exists. She is not fantasy — she is the result of small choices repeated.

Becoming her is not overnight it is daily:
- Show up for yourself
- Honor your boundaries
- Choose kindness toward your body
- Build supportive relationships
- Follow your inner truths
- Create joy with intention
- Allow growth to be slow and sacred

Every time you choose to heal over habit, you step closer to her.

Loving Forward

You once lived hoping to make it through the day. Now you are learning to live toward something. Not just *away* from pain, but *toward* life.

Toward love.
Toward purpose.
Toward meaning.

Loving forward means:
- Loving who you are now
- Loving who you are becoming
- Loving the life you are building
- Loving the world you want to exist in

*This is the evolution: p*ain made you a survivor. Healing made you a seeker. Purpose makes you a teacher. Love makes you whole. You are not finished, you are unfolding.

Chapter 7:

Becoming The You That Tomorrow Needs

<u>PART I</u>

This chapter was about transformation, the slow and sacred evolution that happens after survival. You walked through the question, ***"Who am I now?"*** and discovered that identity is not found, it is rebuilt.

Piece by piece.
Boundary by boundary.
Breath by breath.

You learned that:
- Self-worth is not earned, it's remembered.
- Boundaries are self-love in action.
- Joy can return quietly, like morning light.
- Relationships should feel like home, not harm.
- Triggers do not erase progress.
- Setbacks do not end healing.
- Your voice is rising back to you.
- Your story is not shame, it's strength.
- Pain shaped you, but purpose will use you.
- You are allowed to become brand new.

You are no longer the version who wanted to disappear. You are the version who stayed, even when staying hurt. You are the version who is learning to love herself, to trust herself, to hear her own voice again.

You are becoming someone you are proud to meet each morning.

This is the turning point of your story. The page where surviving ends, and living begins. Where you stop just breathing, and start existing with intention. With joy. With meaning.

WAKE UP TOMORROW

You are no longer building from brokenness; you are building from becoming. And now, you move forward not as the wounded version of you, but as the rising version.

The version who says: "I am here. I stayed. Now what do I do with this life?"

PART II

Learning To Live Forward: From Existing To Thriving

There comes a moment in healing where your past stops defining you and your future begins calling your name.

Not softly, boldly.
Not as pain, as purpose.
Not as survival, as life.

You've walked through darkness with trembling knees, carried pain no child should bear, survived nights no one knew you were fighting, and now you stand on the edge of something new: A life you get to build. A tomorrow you get to choose. A future you are allowed to look forward to.

Thriving isn't about perfection. It's about participation. It's about waking up and saying: "I'm here, so I might as well live." Not just *be alive* but *be living.* This chapter is your permission to step into joy without guilt, into growth without fear, into passion without apology.

Thriving Begins With Small Life

Thriving does not start with grand moments, it starts in the tiny ones most people overlook.

It looks like:
- Waking up and stretching with gratitude
- Drinking your water on purpose
- Playing music that makes you feel
- Smiling at your reflection, even briefly

- Saying "yes" to new experiences
- Taking yourself out into the world
- Laughing without waiting for pain to interrupt
- Finding beauty where you once only saw darkness

Thriving is not an event; it is a lifestyle built slowly. Think of it as planting seeds. Peace seeds. Joy seeds. Self-worth seeds. Future seeds.

The harvest comes later, but the planting begins now. "How do I make it through today?" Living asks: "How can I make today meaningful?"

Thriving asks: "How can I create a life that feels good to inhabit?"

You are leveling up, from survivor, to participant, to creator. Every new choice is a step into the healed world you deserve. And you don't have to fully believe in it yet. You only need to *step toward it.*

Belief will catch up.

Give Yourself Permission To Want More

Trauma teaches you to want less, fewer expectations, fewer hopes, fewer dreams, so disappointment hurts less. Healing teaches you to want again.

Want joy.
Want love.
Want peace.
Want future.
Want fulfillment.

You are allowed to want beautiful things. You are allowed to want laughter, love, home, and purpose. You are allowed to want mornings you're excited for, and nights that feel like peace instead of escape. You are allowed to ask for more. You are allowed to live for more. More is not greedy; more is survival turning into *life.*

Your Past Shaped You

Your Future Will Grow You You are no longer who you were when pain held your hand. You are becoming who you were always meant to be.

Chapter Six is where the light gets loud. Where healing turns into building. Where tomorrow stops being a threat and becomes a promise.

You survived.
Now you grow.
Now you live.
This is the start of thriving.

A Soft Reminder Across All Letters

You do not have to earn love.
You do not need permission to exist.
You are not too broken to be whole.
You are not too late to rebuild.

There is still joy available to you. There is still purpose unfolding. There is still tomorrow waiting to meet you.

You are wanted. You are worthy. You are needed here.

PART III

For The Ones Still Holding On

1. To the Person Who Feels Like a Burden

You think you're too much, but the truth is, you've just been carrying too much alone. You are not a burden. You are a human being with weight that was never meant to be silent. You are allowed to lean. You are allowed to need. You are allowed to ask If someone makes you feel like a burden, they were never meant to hold you.

Real love makes room.
Real support listens.
Real connection doesn't require you to shrink.

You don't have to apologize for breathing.
You don't have to apologize for feeling.
You don't have to apologize for existing.

You are worthy of space, not despite your pain, but during it.

2. To the One Who Survived but Still Hurts

Survival didn't magically erase the memories. Healing didn't immediately remove the triggers. Staying alive didn't end the ache. But it gave you the chance to learn how to live with it, gently, slowly, with grace.

You are not weak for still hurting. You are healing in real time. Healing is not a straight line, it is a spiral, and every time it returns, you meet it with more strength. Every breakdown now has tools.

Every trigger now has breath. Every dark night now has tomorrow waiting.

You survived, and you're still here. Still fighting. Still growing.

That is victory.

3. To the Reader Learning to Love Themselves

You were taught to love everyone else first, to give, give, give, until pieces of you were missing. Now you are learning something new: Love is not something you earn. It is something you are. You do not have to be perfect to be deserving. You do not have to be healed to be lovable. You do not have to be whole to be worthy. Love yourself like you would love a child, with patience, with softness, with forgiveness. Stand in the mirror and speak gently to the reflection that survived hell.

Self-love is not arrogance, it is redemption. It is giving back to the body that carried you through storms. It is honoring the heart that kept beating through heartbreak. It is thanking the soul that stayed.

You are learning to love the one person you once wished away, yourself. And that is holy work.

4. Universal Letter: For Anyone Still Fighting in Silence

Listen to me carefully, the world is better with you in it. Not because of what you do, but because of who you are.

Your smile has value.
Your voice has weight.
Your presence has impact.
Your future has purpose.

WAKE UP TOMORROW

Your existence has meaning.
You may not believe that yet, that's okay.

I will believe for you until you can.

Somewhere ahead, there are mornings waiting for you. New friends waiting to love you. Opportunities waiting to unfold. Joy waiting to burst through you like spring.

You have more story to live.
Stay for it.

Please stay.

"When you don't have the strength to take another step, ask those you love to pull you."

- Author Unknown

Chapter 8:

Closing Summary:
For The Nights You Forget Your Worth

PART 1

This chapter was written for the heart in the shadows, the one who reads between tears and flips these pages like lifelines.

Every letter here is a reminder that:
- You matter even when you feel invisible.
- Childhood wounds can heal in adulthood.
- Pretending you're okay is not the same as being okay.
- Silent healing is still real healing.
- You are not a burden for needing love.
- Surviving does not mean you never hurt.
- You are learning to love yourself in real time.
- Tomorrow is worth waking up for.

These pages were crafted for your darkest hours, the nights where your chest feels tight and your mind whispers endings. When you cannot hear hope, read these letters again. When you doubt your existence, come back here. When you need someone to stay with you through the night, let these words hold your hand.

You are not alone.
Not forgotten.
Not invisible.
Not unlovable.
Not beyond repair.

You are here, and that is a miracle already. This chapter was not just a chapter. It was a blanket. A mirror. A hand on your back. A voice in the dark saying, "Keep breathing."

Hold these letters close. Carry them into your tomorrows. You stayed, and I am so proud of you.

Wake Up Tomorrow The Ending That Became A Beginning

You have journeyed through memory, trauma, survival, healing, purpose, joy, and new life. Now comes the final chapter, the message your entire story has been leading to.

The moment we close the book not with death, but with life.

In the final phase of this book we will explore:
- How to create a tomorrow worth waking up for
- Celebrating your survival as victory
- The promise that healing continues
- Choosing yourself every day
- Claiming your future boldly
- Closing the book with hope, not hurt

The ending of this book is the beginning of your next sunrise.

<u>PART II</u>

Wake Up Tomorrow: Choosing Life On Purpose

You made it here, to the chapter you once believed you'd never live to see. The chapter where survival meets intention. Where breathing becomes living. Where waking up tomorrow is no longer an accident, but a decision made with power.

This chapter is your declaration:
I will not just wake up tomorrow; I will wake up for something.
Not for perfection.
Not for performance.
Not because life is suddenly easy.
But because your life is worth continuing.

Waking up tomorrow is hope in practice.

It means believing that the darkest night is not the whole story.
It means trusting that healing keeps unfolding.
It means choosing yourself, again.

This chapter is not a goodbye. It is the beginning.

<u>1. The Life You Almost Lost is Now the Life You Get to Build</u>

There was a time when you wanted to escape this world. A time you thought the pain was permanent. A time you believed tomorrow wasn't meant for you.

But look at you, still here. Still breathing. Still learning. Still rising.

You lived through chapters you thought would break you.
You crossed seasons you were certain would end you.
You survived moments that tried to convince you not to.

Your survival is not small.
It is monumental.

You remained, and remaining is sacred.

2. You Don't Have to Know the Whole Future — Just the Next Step

Healing does not require a 10-year plan. Purpose does not demand perfection. Life does not unfold all at once. You only need one next step. Wake up tomorrow and do one thing that nurtures you

3. Tomorrow is an Invitation, Not a Threat

For years, tomorrow felt heavy. Unpredictable. Painful. Unwanted.

But now, tomorrow is possibility.

A blank page.
A sunrise waiting.
A chance to experience something new.
Another opportunity to heal deeper.
A fresh doorway into joy.

Imagine waking up tomorrow with expectation, not dread.
Imagine looking forward instead of away.
Imagine opening your eyes and saying: "Thank you for another chance."

You deserve that kind of tomorrow, and you are capable of creating it.

<u>PART III</u>

A Letter to My Future Self:

Dear Future Me,

I hope when you read this, your heart feels lighter than it did in the past. I hope joy sits comfortably inside your chest like it was always meant to live there.

I hope you wake up with purpose, not pain. With anticipation, not dread. With gratitude, not guilt.

I hope you remember how far you've come, the nights you cried quietly into your pillow, the days you carried yourself through exhaustion, the moments you chose life when death whispered soft.

You clawed your way out of darkness that could have swallowed you whole. But you didn't let it.

You stayed.
You survived.
You grew.

And now you're here... reading words written by the girl who once didn't think she'd make it.

Please honor her.
Live well for her.
Love loudly for her.
Laugh freely for her.
Build boundaries for her.
Choose joy for her.

Rest without apology for her.
She kept breathing for you.

I pray your future is full; full of peace that doesn't tremble, love that doesn't wound, rooms where you don't shrink, memories that feel warm, and mornings that welcome you softly.

I pray you look in the mirror and see a woman who is no longer surviving her story but leading others out of theirs. I hope you are proud of who you became; not because you healed perfectly, but because you continued even when afraid.

Keep hoping.
Keep expanding.
Keep believing that you deserve good things, because you do.

And if you ever forget, come back to these words.

With love and gratitude,

The You Who Stayed.

Closing Words Of Love... From Coach Venus

If this book found you in darkness, I hope it became a light. If it met you in silence, I hope it became a voice. If you read it with tears, I hope you now breathe differently. If you held it during a breaking night, I hope you stayed one more day.

You made it here, to the end.
To the beginning.

The chapter you thought would never come.
The tomorrow you once prayed not to see.
The sunrise after the storm.

You stayed. And because you stayed, the world kept a miracle.

You.

I am proud of you.
For surviving.
For healing.
For choosing breath.
For waking up tomorrow.

When days get heavy again, remember this:
You have survived every dark night so far.
You know how to find the light.
You are stronger than that voice that once told you to leave.
You are proof that tomorrow is real.
You are still here.
And because you are here, hope is here too.

This is not where your story ends. It is where it blooms.

Wake up tomorrow.
Not just alive but living.
Loving.
Becoming.

Your life continues.
And it is beautiful already.

Resources & Crisis Support

If you are struggling, please know this: You do not have to face this alone. Help exists. People care. There are voices ready to answer when you reach out.

Use the tools below if you or someone you love is in crisis.

United States Support

- National Suicide & Crisis Lifeline: **Call or Text 988**
- Crisis Text Line: **Text HOME to 741-741**
- National Hope line Network: **1-800-442-4673**
- SAMHSA Treatment Locator: **1-800-662-HELP (4357)**
- The Trevor Project (LGBTQ+ Youth): **1-866-488-7386 / Text START to 678-678**
- Domestic Violence Hotline: **1-800-799-SAFE (7233)**

If you are outside the U.S., search for your local crisis line or emergency service.

If you are in immediate danger, please call emergency services.

Your life matters.
Reach out.
Stay.
Because life is built in small tomorrows.

"Embrace and love all of yourself. Past, present, and future. Forgive yourself quickly and as often as necessary."

- Melody Beattie

ABOUT THE AUTHOR

VENUS CHANDLER

Venus, originally from Akron, Ohio, now resides in Los Angeles, California. She is a proud mother of three and grandmother to five.

With a professional career spanning 36 years in nursing, Venus has dedicated her life to serving others in various medical facilities, including Lynwood Healthcare Center, Los Angeles Community Hospital, and Bay Vista. She has spent the last nine years as a Nurse Manager at Lighthouse Healthcare Center.

VENUS CHANDLER

Venus is a published, number 1 best-selling international author, speaker, life coach, and advocate for survivors of childhood trauma. In 2016, she discovered her true purpose—advocating for women and girls, helping them reclaim their power, purpose, and voice. Once she realized her destiny, she acted, committing herself to uplifting others.

Since then, Venus has embraced her calling, moving freely in the plan God has for her life. She launched her own business, *Kintsugi Transformations Life Coaching Services*, with the goal of helping women develop healthy minds, which she believes are essential for building strong, healthy communities.

Her motto: *"We are strength in numbers!"*

Venus is also the author of her autobiography, *A Silent Scream: My Story, My Truth*, in which she shares her journey of overcoming obstacles and pursuing her dreams. She is living proof that with determination, anyone can discover their purpose and achieve their goals, one step at a time.

MORE BOOKS BY THE AUTHOR

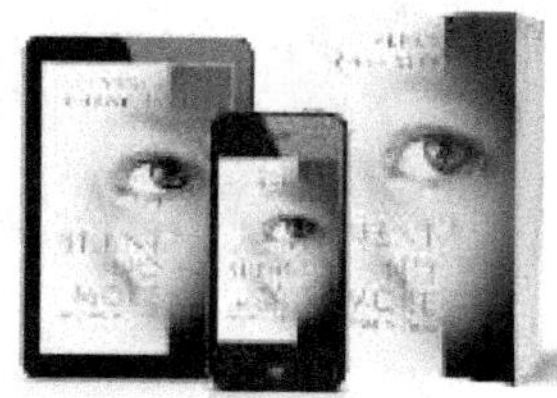

The darkness in her eye represents her past. The light in her eye represents her future. The tear on her face represents the pain she endured. The story represents her freedom and healing. Silent No More is an anthology about childhood trauma. The authors are women who experienced horrific abuse and mistreatment when they should have been protected & cherished. They were violated as minors. They were threatened to keep it secret and forced to keep quiet. Featuring Anjanette Robinson, Brandi Marsh, Carra Braxton, Danniel S. Withers, Jaynel Jones, LaLisa Morgan, Lucretia Y. Hayes, Melanie Rossum, Melissa McGill, Porshe Williams, Tanya DeFreitas, and Vernita Edwards, with a bonus by Terry Chandler. As adults, these women are reclaiming their liberty and victory by telling their truth and they are Silent No More! It's not an easy read, but it was not an easy journey getting to the place of being able to share what they experienced.

VENUS CHANDLER

The story within *A Silent Scream* is far from unique, yet it resonates with countless others who have walked a similar path. In writing this book, Venus Chandler brings attention to the often-overlooked struggles that many face daily. Themes of molestation, rape, addiction, money, and prostitution shaped her journey, but they do not define her. Venus is not a victim of her past; she is a survivor.

This book is written for every broken soul, especially for women who have endured unimaginable trials. It reaches out to those who have wrestled with thoughts of suicide, harbored anger, or dealt with the weight of PTSD. *A Silent Scream* is dedicated to anyone who has had their innocence stolen, suffered sexual abuse, or been harmed by those they trusted to protect them.

Venus Chandler invites readers to reclaim themselves and find their voice. In *A Silent Scream*, she extends permission to release the grip of the past. With each breath and each moment of hope, this book encourages readers to dream again and to become the person they have always longed to be.

Courage.

This is what it takes to pick up the pieces of a shattered heart. Although challenging, these women took a fearless leap and answered the call. It was a call to healing, restoration and trust in God.

Walk with us beyond the echoes of a shattered heart onto the path of healing and redemption.

Courage.

This is what it takes to pick up the pieces of a shattered heart. Although challenging, these women took a fearless leap and answered the call. It was a call to healing and restoration.

Join Coach Venus Chandler and four other courageous women who walk beyond the echoes of a shattered heart onto the path of healing and redemption.